# WHO AM I, LORD?

## Story Devotions for Girls

## Betty Steele Everett

**AUGSBURG** Publishing House • Minneapolis

Manufactured in the United States of America

# Contents

# About This Book

Have you ever thought that, although your face looks the same to everyone you meet, you are really many different people behind it? That's because you have different relationships with the different people in your life. You do not talk to your teachers like you do to your friends. You do not act the same with people older than you are as you do with those who are younger than you. You do not conduct yourself in a strange place, among people you do not know, the same way you do with your friends in a familiar setting. You are even a different person to each member of your family.

So the people you live, study, and play with do not see you the same way. Each one sees you as you are in your relationship with him or her.

Only God sees the whole you. He knows all the people you are, and he loves the complete you. He loves you even when you do wrong, and he sent his Son, Jesus, to die to save you to be his own. He is waiting eagerly to help you when you cannot find your way out of a problem, or when you feel alone and deserted by those you love. Asking God's help and forgiveness is as easy as saying the words and meaning them.

It would take a much thicker book than this to show a girl like you in all of her roles. So this book tries to show girls your age in only a few of their different relationships. Perhaps you will see yourself in them, or see a friend or relative.

It is my prayer that these stories, and the Bible references and prayers with them, will help you to better understand yourself and others. And that they will serve as one guide as you grow, both physically, into a woman, and spiritually, into an adult Christian.

# Big Sister

As Jan came in the front door she saw her younger brother, Kevin, run from her bedroom down the hall. She stepped into his path, and as he tried to push past her, she grabbed his arm.

"What were you doing in my room?" she demanded. "You know you're not allowed in there without my permission! What were you doing?"

"I—I—" Suddenly Kevin burst into tears. "I didn't mean to do it! I didn't mean to! It just happened!"

"What happened?" Jan asked. "You'd better tell me, because I'll find out anyway!"

She was leading him to her room now, opening the door with one hand while she held onto Kevin with the other. She looked quickly around the room, then gasped. There, on the floor by her desk where she had left it, was the library book she had borrowed yesterday.

Jan let go of Kevin's hand to pick up the book, and he dashed out of the room. She heard his bedroom door slam.

But Jan was staring at the page where the library book had fallen open. "It's ripped! He ripped this page with the picture on it! Oh, it's torn all the way too!"

She ran from the room and pounded on her brother's door. "Kevin! You let me in! You ripped my library book!"

For a moment there was silence, then the door slowly opened. Kevin stood there with tears on his cheeks, holding onto his old teddy bear—the one he never bothered with anymore.

"I didn't mean to!" he sobbed. "I was just looking at the pretty pictures, and then I picked the book up, and it started to fall, and I grabbed it, and—and it tore! I didn't mean to hurt your book."

"Well, you did hurt it!" Jan snapped. "And it's a library book! That means I'm responsible for it! I have to pay a fine if it gets lost or torn! And I've had a perfect record at the library till now too! This will ruin it! Wait till I tell Mom!"

She took the book and marched to the kitchen where her mother was getting dinner. "Look what Kevin did to my library book!" She held the book so her mother could see the torn page.

"I didn't mean to!" Kevin had followed her and was crying again.

"But you did do it, didn't you?" his mother asked gently.

Kevin nodded.

"Well, I'm sure the library will understand," Jan's

mother said. "I'm sure Mrs. Rogers has seen accidents before."

"Kevin did it!" Jan said. "He ought to have to tell Mrs. Rogers! It's bad enough it goes on my record—he at least ought to be the one who tells her what happened and that he's sorry!"

Her mother looked at her and then at Kevin. "Do you really think he should?" she asked Jan. "He's pretty small—and it was an accident!"

"I don't care!" Jan insisted. "It was his fault!"

Her mother hesitated, then said, "All right, if you feel that way. Kevin, I'll take you to the library tomorrow, and you can tell Mrs. Rogers you're sorry about the book and that it was your fault, not Jan's."

Kevin swallowed hard. "Do I have to?" he asked in a low voice.

"Of course you do!" Jan said. "It was your fault! You shouldn't have touched my book!" She hurried from the room. "That will teach him a lesson!" she told herself.

During dinner both Jan and Kevin were quiet. After dinner, Jan decided to call her best friend, Judi, and talk about the next day's math assignment.

Judi and Jan talked a long time. "Do you know what my brother did?" Jan asked. She told her friend about the library book. "Mom is making him go to the library tomorrow and apologize to Mrs. Rogers so she'll know it wasn't my fault."

"Wow!" Judi said. "He'll never forget that!" She giggled. "Remember when we were about his age and were playing ball and the ball hit those flowers in Mrs. Wilson's yard and broke two of her best tulips right off?"

Jan laughed. "I remember! Mom made us go apologize to her, and was I ever scared! I was sure she would hit us or yell at us or something! I thought she would hate us for doing something that bad!"

Judi giggled again. "Remember how we held hands and kept telling each other we weren't scared? If you hadn't been with me, I would have been twice as scared!"

"But Kevin has to go alone!" Jan said suddenly. "I wonder if he feels as scared of Mrs. Rogers as we felt of Mrs. Wilson."

"Probably," Judi said. "Everything's scary when you're that little. I guess things are scary no matter how old you are, though. But your Mom knows what she's doing, so if she said he had to do it, it's all right. Mrs. Rogers is nice—she won't yell at him or anything. She'll be as nice to him as Mrs. Wilson was to us. Mrs. Wilson's one of my favorite people now."

"But Kevin hardly knows Mrs. Rogers. He doesn't know how nice she is," Jan said. "And I was so scared that day going to see Mrs. Wilson." She remembered how her heart had pounded as she and Judi had walked up the steps to Mrs. Wilson's front door. Her mouth had been dry, but her hands had been sweating. "And I'm the one who wanted Mom to make Kevin go!" she said.

"But your Mom wouldn't do it if she didn't think it was right," Judi argued.

"I guess so," Jan agreed. But she hung up soon after that and went to her room to think.

"It is Kevin's fault," she told herself. "And Mrs. Rogers won't really be angry with him." But she kept remembering how frightened she had been with Mrs. Wilson, and how small Kevin was. And he would be facing Mrs. Rogers all alone.

At last Jan decided what to do. She said a quick prayer, asking Jesus to help her. Then she found her mother in the kitchen. "Mom, would it be OK with you if I went with Kevin tomorrow to tell Mrs. Rogers about the book?" she asked.

Her mother nodded. "I think it would be fine, if it's all right with Kevin."

Jan went back and knocked on her brother's door. When he opened it, she saw he had been looking at the damaged book.

"Kevin, I've been thinking. It's—well, I shouldn't have left my book out like I did, and it is on my library card, and—well, if you want me to, I'll go with you tomorrow to tell Mrs. Rogers we're sorry."

Kevin's face lighted, and he smiled for the first time since the book had been torn. "Would you? Would you really go with me? And not be mad at me anymore? Oh, Jan, I was so scared! And you were so mad at me. . . . But if you're not mad and you go with me, I won't be afraid any more. I'm not afraid of anything when you're with me! But when I'm alone, I'm afraid lots of times."

Jan looked at him in surprise. He was looking at her as though she could do anything in the world! "Why," she thought, "he thinks just because I'm bigger I can take care of him no matter what!"

Jan looked away. She had not realized how important it was to be a big sister, what a responsibility it was. She had not been a very good example for Kevin today.

"But I can be!" Jan thought. "I'll try to do better with him from now on."

She smiled and reached down for Kevin's hand. "I'll go with you tomorrow, Kevin, but I can't always

12

be with you. Let's get out your Bible story book. I want to read you the part about how Jesus will be with you all the time. He will be with you wherever you are, even if you're all alone. Jesus is your best friend! He loves you—and so do I!"

Kevin smiled. "And you're my next best friend— 'cause you're my big sister! And we love each other."

> And now I give you a new com- mandment: love one another. As I have loved you, so you must love one another.
>
> John 13:34

*Help me, Lord Jesus, to understand that "things" are not as important as people. Help me to treat the people in my family with love, so that they will always know how much I care for them. Amen.*

# I Never Get to Do Anything

"Time for bed, Kathy!"

Kathy looked up as her mother came to the door of the family room. "Oh, Mom, not yet! I want to watch this next TV show! And Suzy doesn't have to go to bed for ages! Why do I always have to go to bed so early?"

"Because you're five years younger than Suzy," her mother said patiently. "Come on, now, don't stall till you get interested in that new program."

"It's not fair!" Kathy said angrily. "It's not fair! Suzy gets to do everything! I never get to do anything! It's not fair!" She stamped out of the room and down the hall to her bedroom, still muttering, "It's not fair!"

In her room, Kathy flung herself onto the bed. "Suzy gets to do anything she wants! She gets to go

14

anywhere she wants too! She's Mom and Dad's favorite! They don't care about me!"

She was in bed when her mother came in to say good-night.

"Did you say your prayers?" her mother asked.

"I'll do it!" Kathy said. "Do you ask Suzy that too?"

"Sometimes," her mother answered. "And I always did when she was your age."

"I bet!" Kathy said softly as her mother left the room. "I just bet!"

She got out of bed to say her prayers, but tonight they did not comfort her. She hurried through them and got back into bed, still angry.

The next morning Kathy was eating breakfast when Suzy came into the kitchen. "Mom," Suzy said, "is it OK if I stay after school tonight to help Joe decorate the gym for our class party? He'll bring me home."

"I guess so. Tell Joe to drive carefully," their mother said.

"See?" Kathy snapped. "See? Suzy gets to ride in a car a grown-up isn't driving, but do I? No way! I never get to do anything!"

"You get to act like a brat!" Suzy snapped. "You act like a baby!"

"Girls!" Their mother's tone stopped them both. Kathy glared at Suzy as she left.

Later, as she walked to school with her friend Emily, Kathy was still complaining. "You're lucky you're an only child!" Kathy said.

"I wish I had a sister like Suzy," Emily said. "I like her."

"You wouldn't if she got to do things and you didn't!"

15

That afternoon when Kathy got home she was surprised to see Suzy there. "I thought you were staying after school to help decorate the gym. How come you're home?" Kathy asked.

"Mom called me at school last period. She said Grandma fell and they took her to the hospital. Mom had to go there. She wanted me to come home and be here to tell you and to get dinner. Mom didn't know how long she'd have to stay at the hospital."

"I don't need anyone to baby-sit with me!" Kathy said. "Why didn't Mom call and tell me too?"

Suzy sighed. "She didn't have time! And she wanted to be sure I'd get Dad's dinner 'cause he has that church board meeting tonight and only has an hour to eat and get there."

"Well, I hope Gram's OK." Kathy said.

Suzy put an arm around her. "I'm sure she'll be all right. They may have to do surgery though. So I'd better get to work here. Mom said she hadn't vacuumed the living room yet either."

Kathy started for her bedroom as the telephone rang. "Maybe that's Mom!" she said as she grabbed the receiver. But it was not her mother; it was Emily.

"Kathy, come over right away! My uncle just brought me a puppy! It's so cute! You have to see it right away!"

"A puppy? Oh, Emily!" Kathy stopped. "But I don't know if I can come. . . ." She looked over at Suzy with a question in her eyes.

Suzy nodded. "I'll call you if I hear from Mom."

Kathy ran to hug her sister. "Thanks, Suzy!"

When Kathy returned home for dinner an hour later, she was glad to see her mother there. "How's Gram?"

"She had emergency surgery to set her hip," her mother said, "but she came through it just fine. I'm going to eat and go back."

"We'll do the dishes, Mom," Suzy said. "Joe called, and they got the gym decorated all right." She laughed. "He said it looked almost as good as if I'd helped!"

"When can we see Gram?" Kathy asked.

"You can come with me tomorrow since it's Saturday," her mother said.

But the next morning when they were standing at the elevator in the hospital, a man in a uniform stopped them.

"I'm sorry," he said, looking at Kathy, "but children under 14 are not allowed upstairs unless it's one of their parents who is sick."

"But it's Gram!" Kathy said. "You have to let me go up!" She could feel her throat getting tight the way it always did when she was going to cry.

Just then a new voice spoke. "It's all right, Ed."

Kathy turned to see Grandma's doctor standing beside them. The guard nodded, and Kathy smiled.

"Thanks, Dr. Smith. I want to see Gram really bad. Why don't they let people under 14 upstairs?"

The doctor smiled. "They can create quite a disturbance and upset the other patients. It's a good rule, but I know you won't do that. So you go on up and see your grandma."

As the elevator door closed, Kathy said, "It's terrible not to be able to do things because of your age."

"Time will take care of it, dear," her mother said, smiling. "Don't worry!"

"But that doesn't help me now! I wouldn't have

17

gotten to see Gram at all if Dr. Smith hadn't come along and said it was all right!"

Kathy was still upset and angry when they got to her grandmother's room. Even seeing Gram did not make her feel better.

They had talked only a few minutes when Gram said, "Suzy, would you and your mother go get me some fresh ice water, please? The nurses are so busy they don't have time to keep it cold."

When Kathy and her grandmother were alone, Gram said, "What's bothering you, Kathy? I can tell something's wrong. Out with it."

"I never get to do anything!" Kathy said. "Suzy does everything, but I couldn't even have come up here if Dr. Smith hadn't made them let me! But that guard wasn't going to stop Suzy!"

Her grandmother sighed. "It's hard to be young. But remember last night—Suzy gave up the fun of decorating the gym for a party to go home and get dinner for you and your father because your mother was here."

Kathy nodded. She did not see what that had to do with her never being allowed to do the things Suzy got to do.

"Do you think Suzy really wanted to do that?" Gram asked.

Kathy shrugged. She had not thought about whether or not Suzy had wanted to come home to get dinner. "But she had to, Gram. There wasn't anyone else but me, and I can't get a whole dinner myself."

Gram smiled. "By the time you're Suzy's age you'll be able to, though. But I don't imagine Suzy would choose to get a meal instead of decorating the gym if she had a choice, do you? She was being what we call

18

a 'mature and responsible' person. Someone your mother could count on. Every age has its responsibilities—and its limitations. Right now you only see the limitations. As you grow, the limitations change to privileges. But responsibilities and privileges go together."

Kathy sat quietly, thinking. She had gotten to go see Emily's puppy yesterday, but Suzy had not gotten to do what she wanted because she was the oldest and responsible for getting dinner. Kathy knew going to Emily's had been more fun than staying home to cook.

"I guess I never thought of it like that, Gram." She reached over and took the old woman's hand. "Thanks. I guess I haven't been acting very grown-up lately, but I'm going to do better. And I'm going to enjoy the privileges I have right now—so I can be responsible enough to have more when I get to Suzy's age."

"Well done, you good and faithful servant!" said his master. "You have been faithful in managing small amounts, so I will put you in charge of large amounts. Come on in and share my happiness!"

Matthew 25:21

*I want to be a responsible and faithful person, Lord. I want to be someone who has earned privileges and who can be counted on for help when I am needed. Give me patience to wait for the privileges that older people have and to work to earn them for myself. Thank you. Amen.*

# Grown-Up

When she heard Bonnie's whistle outside, Marsha grabbed her backpack with the sandwiches in it. "Got to go, Mom! See you later!"

"Wait a minute," her mother said. "Where are you and Bonnie going today?"

"Just for a bike ride!" Marsha wished her mother would not ask so many questions about what she did.

"I know, but exactly where, dear?"

"Mom! Can't you trust me? I'm not going to get into any trouble! Bonnie's mother never asks her where she's going! Her mother treats her like a grown-up and trusts her! Why can't you do that?"

Marsha's mother started to put her arms around Marsha's shoulders, but Marsha pulled away. Her mother pretended not to notice. "Because I am responsible for you, Marsha. And I need to know where you are in case I need you. I'm afraid that's the rule in this house—your father and I have to know where all of you children are going when you leave, who you are with, and when you can be expected back. Even Ellen tells us, and she's in junior college."

"Oh, all right! We're going to ride our bikes out to the farm the church got for its camp and retreat center. We'll explore and eat our lunch there."

"Then you should be home by about three o'clock," her mother said. "Can I count on you being back by then?"

"Yes!" Marsha slipped her backpack on and rushed outside. She was glad Bonnie had not come inside to hear how many questions her mother asked.

"I bet you had to tell your mother everything!" Bonnie teased as the girls began to pedal away from the house. "I didn't! I'm no baby!"

"Neither am I!" Marsha said. "I'll race you!" She speeded up before Bonnie could ask any questions. If Bonnie thought she had not had to tell her mother where they were going, maybe she would stop teasing her.

Later the girls pedaled more slowly along the state route that led to the old farm their church owned. A year from now it would be a place for groups to meet and hold retreats. The farm had been left to them by a member who had not lived on it for years. There was only an old shed on the land now, and it would soon be torn down.

The girls walked their bikes up the rutted lane leading to where there had once been a house. Now everything was overgrown and littered. Only a few flowers showed that once someone had cared for the ground.

"We'd better cover our bikes and lunches to keep

21

the sun off," Bonnie said. "I don't want the paint on mine to fade or my lunch to spoil. We can use some of this brush."

In a few minutes the bikes were shaded, and the girls began to walk around the area. They tried to imagine where each new structure would be when the camp was all ready. There would be a big building with rooms to sleep in on the top floor. Downstairs there would be a dining room, kitchen, and two meeting rooms.

"Dad says the workers are going to make a big fireplace in the main room," Bonnie said. "They're going to use stones from the farm for it!"

"Then let's look for big stones!" Marsha said excitedly. "We can make a pile of them, and when it's time to make the fireplace, we'll have helped!"

"Bet I find a bigger one than you do!" Bonnie said.

"Bet you don't!" Marsha answered.

The girls separated, each looking for big stones that could be used in the fireplace. Suddenly Marsha saw what looked like a lot of big stones just a few feet ahead. She laughed. "I'll take the biggest one before I tell Bonnie they're here! Then we can take all we want."

Marsha was almost to the stones when she felt the ground give way under her. She flung her arms wildly to try to keep her balance, but it was no use. Marsha felt herself falling forward and down. She landed on her side with a thud. A sharp pain went through her right arm as she tried to cushion her fall.

"Oh!" Marsha moaned. "Where am I?" She tried to get up, but she could not use the arm that hurt. "It must be broken!" Now Marsha was afraid. She did not know where she was, and she could not use her arm. "Bonnie!" she shouted. "Help me! Bonnie!"

She looked up and saw the hole into which she had fallen. Sunlight came through it, but it was dark all around her. She guessed she was about six feet below the opening. Marsha struggled to her feet and reached up her good left arm. Her fingers were a long way from the top. "Bonnie!" she screamed. "Bonnie!"

"Marsha! Where are you?" Bonnie's voice sounded far away.

"Down here! I fell and I can't get out! Help me!"

"I can't see you!" Bonnie shouted back.

"I'm down in a hole! I hurt my arm! Help me!"

"I'm coming!"

Marsha watched the hole above her. Suddenly it was dark; something had blocked out the sun. A shower of dirt and small stones began to fall around her.

"Ohh!" came Bonnie's startled voice. Then Bonnie was falling toward Marsha. The hole was much bigger now.

Bonnie landed partly on Marsha, but she was not hurt. "Where are we?" Bonnie whispered. She sounded as frightened as Marsha felt.

"It must be an old well," Marsha said. "I read once how people who had wells and didn't want them any more filled them in and covered them over. This one must only have been partly filled. At least it's dry!"

"But we can't get out!" Bonnie said. "Marsha, what are we going to do? We'll starve or die of thirst!" She began sobbing wildly and clawing at the sides of the well. But her hands could not reach the top, and she

24

could not get a grip on the old walls. They were covered with a slippery green slime.

"Stop it!" Marsha ordered. "Sit down!"

"But we're going to die! No one will ever find us till it's too late! We even hid our bikes! And we didn't bring our lunches with us! Marsha, we're going to die right here in this well!"

"No, we're not!" Marsha said. "My mother knows we were coming here. She expects me back by three o'clock. When I don't show up, she'll call your mom. Then they'll get in the car and drive right out here. They'll find our bikes, and then they'll find us. All we have to do is wait."

"I thought you said you didn't have to tell your mother where you were going," Bonnie said.

"Well, I did! And I'm no baby, either!"

"Do you really think they'll find us soon?" Bonnie asked.

"About 3:30," Marsha said. "Let's pray that they'll come even sooner."

When the girls had finished praying, they sat on the damp ground. They leaned against each other.

"I'm glad your mom asked you where we were going," Bonnie said slowly. "My mother wouldn't have known where to look for me. They might not have found us."

"I'm glad too," Marsha said. For the first time, she really was glad. "I guess telling people where you are going is being smart. And being smart is being grown-up! I'm going to tell Mom I understand that now."

"Me too," Bonnie said. "I'm going to tell Mom where I'm going from now on—even if she doesn't ask me."

Marsha nodded and looked around her. "I think we've found enough stones for the whole fireplace too! This old well can be the fireplace—and it will always remind us of how we learned to be grown-up."

> Children, it is your Christian duty to obey your parents, for this is the right thing to do. "Respect your father and mother" is the first commandment that has a promise added: "so that all may go well with you, and you may live a long time in the land."
> Ephesians 6:1-3

*I want so much to be grown-up, Lord, and to be treated like an adult. Please help me to remember that to be treated like a grown-up, I must act like one. Amen.*

# Lucy's Pledge

Lucy stood in the doorway of the Sunday school room the friendly superintendent had pointed out to her. All around her were boys and girls her age, but none of them paid any attention to her. They were all talking and laughing in their own little groups.

"All right, class!" called a plump, middle-aged woman with a bright smile. "Time to get started on today's lesson. Everyone around the table now!" Then she noticed Lucy. "Hello, there. You're new here, aren't you? I'm Mrs. Morgan. Welcome to our church. What's your name?"

"Lucy Jenson." Lucy had meant to speak it out strongly, so the others would have to know who she was, but it came out almost a whisper. She felt her face getting red. Wouldn't she ever learn to make

27

new friends when her father was moved by his company? This wasn't the first time she'd been a stranger.

"Class, this is Lucy Jenson from. . . ."

"Vermont," Lucy said, and this time her voice was too loud.

The teacher rattled off the names of the others, and each one nodded or waved. "You can sit next to Jackie," Mrs. Morgan said. "Jackie's our best Bible verse memorizer."

Lucy sat down next to the strange girl. "Hi," she said.

"Hi." Jackie handed her a book. "This is our lesson book—this is today's lesson."

"Thanks."

After that Jackie said no more to her, and Lucy did not take part in any of the class's discussion of the lesson.

"I wish I knew some way to make them want to be my friends," Lucy thought as she listened to the talk around her. "Some way to make them like me, even if I am new!"

Then, a few minutes before the bell rang, Mrs. Morgan said, "I want to report to you on the pledges you made last week for our class's contribution to the mission in the Philippines. Last week you each wrote down the amount you wanted to pledge, to be paid in two more weeks. But when I added them together, they were still $20 short of what we said we would like our class to give."

Lucy looked questioningly at Jackie, who whispered, "We pledged $50 from our class to help the missionaries—every class is making a pledge. But I guess we didn't say we'd each give enough. No one pledged more than $5, probably."

Suddenly Lucy knew what to do to be accepted here. She raised her hand. "Mrs. Morgan, I'd like to pledge the $20. You said it was due in two weeks?"

Everyone was looking at her, and it made Lucy feel good. Now they were noticing her!

"Why, Lucy, that's—well, wonderful, but do you think your parents . . . I mean, perhaps you should check with them first." Mrs. Morgan was obviously confused.

Lucy shook her head. "It'll be my money."

The bell rang then, and Jackie said, "Some of us sit together in church—our folks let us as long as we don't act up or anything. Want to sit with us?"

Lucy smiled and nodded. It was working already! Why hadn't she ever seen before what to do to be accepted right away?

It was not until the next evening that Lucy began to think about where she might get the money she had pledged in Sunday school. "Mom," she said as she helped with the dishes after dinner, "how can I get $20?"

Her older brother looked at her in surprise. "What do you need so much for?" Bob asked. "You've only been in school one day!"

"It's not for school." Lucy explained about the pledge she had made for the mission.

"Why did you pledge so much, dear?" her mother asked. "Of course we must all give all we can, but $20 is a lot for someone your age."

"I thought they needed it," Lucy said. She did not want to mention that she had done it more to get the others to notice her and be her friends. It had worked, though, Lucy told herself. Jackie had met her part way to school this morning, and she had sat with Jackie's friends at noon. Of course no one had mentioned the pledge, but Lucy knew that was the real reason the others were so friendly.

"You'd better give her the money," Bob told their mother.

"Right now I can't afford to," Lucy's mother said. "Moving costs a lot."

"But she'll never be able to raise that much herself in two weeks," Bob said.

"Yes, I will!" Lucy insisted.

But a week later, as she went into church, Lucy had to admit Bob had been right. "I should never have pledged so much," she thought miserably. "I'll never have enough to pay it! Oh, why did we have to leave Vermont and move to Iowa?"

Jackie looked at her strangely, Lucy thought, as they worked on the lesson together. After church, Jackie said, "Something's wrong, Lucy. What is it? Can I help?"

Lucy looked down at the ground. "If I tell you, you'll hate me!" She sighed. "But everyone'll know next week! I don't have the money for my mission pledge!"

"Oh."

"I should never have made such a big pledge!" Lucy said. "I wanted you all to notice me—and to like me! I thought if I made that pledge you would. I thought my folks could lend me the money, but they can't right now. I've only got $5. Oh, Jackie, everyone's going to hate me!"

"No, they won't," Jackie said slowly. "And I'm sorry you thought we wouldn't be your friends unless you made a big pledge. We would have liked you anyway." Then her face brightened. "Come home with me for lunch! It'll make you feel better. On Sundays we always have Gram's unmaple syrup on waffles."

Lucy stared at her. "Your grandmother's what?"

Jackie laughed. "Unmaple syrup! Gram makes it with corn cobs and sugar!"

"Corn cobs and sugar? Ugh!" Lucy made a face. "It sounds terrible! Now if it were real Vermont maple syrup. . . ."

"Bet you can't tell the difference!" Jackie said. "Do you have any real maple syrup at home?"

"Sure, but—"

"Bring it! We'll blindfold you, and I bet you can't tell which is which!"

"I bet I can! Nothing tastes like maple syrup!"

"Gram's does!"

Lucy hurried home. Her parents agreed she could go to Jackie's, and she quickly changed her clothes. In the kitchen, she got a small bottle of maple syrup. It had been made by neighbors in Vermont; she had watched them do it.

"And Jackie thinks I won't know the difference!" Lucy tasted a little on her finger and smiled.

Jackie's family was waiting for her. "We'll blindfold you," Jackie said. "Then we'll put Gram's syrup on one waffle and yours on the other. You have to tell which is which!"

Lucy laughed. "That'll be easy!"

When she took her first bite of waffle, Lucy smiled. "This is mine."

"Try the other one," Jackie ordered as Lucy started to take off the blindfold.

Lucy took another bite, then paused. "This tastes almost the same—but it can't!" She took another bite, and then a bite of the first sample. She was getting

31

confused, but she had to make a decision. "The first one!"

Jackie was nodding as Lucy took off the blindfold. "I didn't think you could do it."

"I almost couldn't!" Lucy turned to Jackie's grandmother. "How do you make that? Jackie said you used corn cobs, but I don't believe that!"

"It's true, dear," Jackie's grandmother said. "We have lots of corn cobs in Iowa—but not many maple trees! You boil the cobs in enough water to cover them for about two hours. Then you strain off the liquid, and mix one cup of sugar to two cups of liquid. Then you just cook it slowly until it's slightly thick like syrup. If you used white sugar, you'd have a light syrup; brown sugar makes a darker syrup."

Lucy shook her head. "Corn cobs! I can't believe it!"

She and Jackie were finishing the dishes later when Lucy had her idea. "Jackie, we can make your grandmother's 'unmaple syrup' and sell it to get the money for our mission pledges! I bet not many people really make it, and we could give them a free taste. . . ."

Jackie's eyes lighted. "We've got lots of cobs, and Gram could help us after school tomorrow night! We'll put it in jars and sell it!"

"Let's tell the other kids!" Lucy said. "They can bring jars and help sell it! We'll make more than the class's pledge!"

Jackie grinned. "And then no one will care who pledged how much! Lucy, it's a great idea! I'm sure glad your family moved to Iowa!"

Lucy smiled back. "So am I!" she said, and for the first time, she really meant it.

Keep on loving one another as Christian brothers. Remember to welcome strangers in your homes. There were some who did that and welcomed angels without knowing it.

Hebrews 13:1-2

*Thank you, Lord, for Christian friends who love me even when I am a stranger and do selfish and foolish things. Help me to be a friend to strangers the way I want them to be friends to me. Amen.*

# Ginny's Pax Cake

Usually Ginny loved going to see her grandparents. They lived in a big apartment building and had a tiny porch that looked out over the street below. The porch was her favorite place at night when the traffic moved and the street lights changed from red to green.

But today, sitting in the back seat of the car with her brother, Ginny did not feel like doing anything.

"It's all Carol's fault!" she told herself again. "She started the fight yesterday! She's the one who took her Barbie doll and its things and went home! She's the one who said she'd never speak to me again!" She tried to forget that she had been just as angry when she shouted, "And I'll never speak to you again, either!"

This was the first time Ginny could remember going away overnight without a special good-bye to Carol. But she had sat straight in her seat and not even looked as they passed Carol's house.

"If that's the way she wants it," Ginny told herself, "that's fine with me!"

Joe, her brother, was watching her now. "You're sure quiet. Want to play the alphabet game with the signs?"

"OK," Ginny said. It was her favorite game for trips—trying to find the letters of the alphabet in order on the big signs along the road—but today she didn't care if they played or not.

"There's an A!" Joe shouted. "And a B and a C!"

Joe won easily, and Ginny was glad when they finally arrived in the big parking lot that guests at the apartment building used. Soon they were riding up in the elevator.

"Hello!" Ginny's grandparents met them at the elevator. Ginny threw her arms around her grandmother's neck.

Inside, the apartment smelled of turkey and pumpkin pie.

"It's not Thanksgiving, Grandma," Ginny said, laughing. "I bet Carol would like. . . ." She stopped, remembering that she and Carol weren't friends any more.

"Bring her along next time," her grandmother said. "Now, do you want to help me in the kitchen?"

"Sure!"

Dinner was fun, and Ginny almost forgot about her fight with Carol. After dinner she went out onto the small porch to watch the traffic before she had to go to bed.

The next morning Ginny was up before her parents

or Joe. In the kitchen she found her grandmother mixing a cake.

"Hello, Early Bird," her grandmother said, smiling. "How'd you sleep?"

"Fine."

"Good. Now, tell me what you and Carol have been up to lately. You've hardly mentioned her."

"I—I don't know," Ginny said. She looked down at the floor instead of at her grandmother.

"You don't sound as though you two were still friends. What happened?"

"It's all her fault!" Ginny said angrily. "She started it! Then she went home and said she would never speak to me again in her whole life!"

"And what did you say to her?" her grandmother asked gently.

"I—I told her I'd never speak to her again either!"

"I see. So it's partly your fault too, isn't it? And now you miss Carol—and you wonder if she misses you."

Ginny nodded. Her grandmother was right; she had been wondering if Carol missed her too.

"You can find out today when you go home," her grandmother said. "All you have to do is ask her. You can go over or call on the telephone."

"But I can't! She started it! I can't talk to her first!"

Her grandmother looked thoughtful. "I think what you need is a 'pax cake.'"

"A what kind of cake?" Ginny asked.

"*Pax* is the Latin word for 'peace.' You bake a small cake, then take it to whomever you have been angry with, and offer them half of it. As you eat it together, it means you are friends again—sharing peace like you've shared the cake."

"I never saw a 'pax cake.'"

36

"My mother told me about them when I was your age. They were a custom in England a long time ago. Mother said they had them at their church one year during Holy Week before Easter. She baked several for me while I was growing up. She always said she didn't see why it had to be Holy Week before you could share a 'pax cake.'"

Ginny thought about it. Carol loved cake. "Could you make me one, Grandma?"

"Right now. There's enough batter, and I have just the right size pan."

When her parents were ready to leave that afternoon, Ginny's grandmother handed her a small box. "I wrote 'Peace' on it in pink icing," she whispered.

Ginny held the box tightly all the way home. She looked at Carol's house as they passed; Carol was sitting alone on the front steps, and Ginny thought she looked sad.

At home Ginny stopped only long enough to leave her overnight bag and be sure the pax cake was in her pocket before hurrying to Carol's house.

"Hi," she said as she went up the drive.

"Who said you could come in my yard?" Carol demanded.

Ginny almost turned around, but the box with the pax cake was heavy in her pocket, so she paid no attention to Carol's angry tone.

"I have something—a 'pax cake'—for us to eat together."

"What kind of a cake is that?"

Ginny explained as she opened the box to show Carol the small cake with 'Peace' in pink icing. It looked delicious.

"We eat it together, and then we're friends again," Ginny said. "Do you want some?"

"I guess so."

Ginny divided the cake, carefully giving Carol the slightly larger piece.

They sat together, eating the cake in silence. Then, brushing the last crumbs from her lap, Carol stood up. "That was good. I—I'm glad we're friends again now. I missed you. I couldn't even remember what we fought about. We can be friends forever now."

Ginny giggled. "Then Grandma will have to make a really big cake—and put 'Ginny and Carol—Friends Forever' on it!"

> Happy are those who work for peace; God will call them his children!
>
> Matthew 5:9

*Lord, please help me to forgive people when they hurt me and to remember how much you have forgiven all of us. Thank you for dying for my sins. Amen.*

# Stranger in Class

April, along with the rest of her Sunday school classmates, was sitting at her desk in their classroom when Mr. Aiken, the superintendent, came in. He had his arm around a boy their age.

"This is Bruce Whitman, class," Mr. Aiken said. "His family just moved here, and he wants to be part of your class."

April stared at the stranger. Some of the others giggled quietly. Bruce was wearing a pair of faded jeans and a white T-shirt. He had on a coat from an old suit. It was much too large for him, and the sleeves had been turned back and sewed there. His blue canvas shoes were scuffed, and there was a small hole along the little toe of the right one.

"He looks like he moved from the city dump," whispered Angie, the girl sitting next to April. She put her hand over her mouth to keep from laughing.

"He's clean!" April whispered back. "And his hair's combed!" But it *was* hard not to laugh.

Bruce looked them over with his big, brown eyes. There was no smile on his face, and he said nothing.

"We're happy to have you, Bruce," Mr. Thomas said. The teacher pointed to an empty desk. "You can sit there. We're just beginning our lesson."

Bruce nodded without speaking and sat down where Mr. Thomas told him. He kept his eyes down and did not look at anyone.

The lesson did not go well. No one seemed interested in the Bible story and its meaning for today. April knew everyone was wondering about Bruce. He did look out of place here where everyone had on good clothes.

When the bell rang to end the class, Bruce jumped up quickly and hurried to the door. He was the first one out of the room.

"Isn't he something?" a boy named Ron asked in a low voice. "Where'd he ever get that coat?"

"From his dad, it looks like," Angie said. Everyone laughed except April, but she too was wondering where the coat had come from. It must have belonged to someone else first.

During the next week April did not see Bruce. School was out for the summer, but the church gang met at the playground every day.

"Wonder what happened to that Bruce?" Ron said one day as they sat on the grass under a tree. "He was something else!"

"He wasn't in church after Sunday school," Angie said. "I wanted to see what his folks looked like!"

"Christians shouldn't laugh at people's clothes!"

41

April snapped. "Bruce can't help it if he's poor! They must be poor."

"Do you think he'll come back this Sunday?" Ron asked. "He sure is different!"

"He probably got that message!" April said. "The way he ran out after Sunday school was over. . . . But he must be a Christian, or he wouldn't have come in the first place! It's hard to come to a new church at all, and if your folks don't come with you, it must be a whole lot harder!"

"Why'd he pick our church?" Ron asked. "I don't think he lives around here. There are a lot of churches he could go to."

"Like the one downtown," Angie said. "That's for people like Bruce. They have lots of old clothes to give them. Mom sends all our old stuff down there."

April said no more. She did not think Bruce would come back to their Sunday school, but when she reached her classroom on Sunday morning, there he was. He was wearing the same clothes he had been wearing the Sunday before. April hesitated outside the classroom door. No one else was there yet, but Bruce had seen her. She would have to go in.

"Hi, Bruce," she said. "You're early." She could not think of anything else to say.

Bruce's face turned pink. "Aren't you allowed to be early? I mean, I just wanted to look at this book. I saw it last week—it has pictures of Jesus in it, and I wanted to see if they were like. . . ." He stopped suddenly, blushing even more. Then he closed the thick book of Bible stories and put it back on the side table where it belonged.

"Like what?" April asked.

"Nothing!" Bruce shoved a folded piece of paper into his pocket.

"Bruce Whitman, let me see that!" April tried to sound firm. What if Bruce had torn a picture from the book?

Bruce shrugged. He unfolded the paper and handed it to April. It was a sketch of Jesus with a lamb on his shoulder and a small boy holding his other hand. The face of Jesus was strong, yet it had a tender smile.

April stared at the picture. "Bruce, did you draw this? It's good!"

"It's not finished," Bruce said. "It's just a sketch. The real painting will be on good paper. Jesus will have a white robe with blue trim on it, and the lamb will be just a little gray, and the boy will have dark hair, and. . . ." Bruce's voice got more excited as he talked.

"Bruce, you have to finish it!" April said. She was as excited as Bruce now. "It would look perfect here in our classroom! I'll get a frame. . . ."

"Here!" Bruce looked surprised. "But I don't think the others. . . ."

"Leave it to me! I have an idea."

The others came in before April could say anything more. They were all talking and laughing, and no one stopped to give Bruce more than a quick "Hi." It was almost as though he wasn't even there, April thought angrily. But they'd find out!

Later, when the group was standing outside between Sunday school and church, April said, "What's wrong with all of you? You've never treated anyone like you're treating Bruce! And you don't even know him!"

43

"What's to know?" Ron asked.

Angie giggled. "Maybe April likes him! But you'll have to get different clothes to be like him, April—old ones!"

"God doesn't care about clothes!" April snapped. But she knew everyone else did. Until she had seen Bruce's picture, she had been as bad as the others!

The next Sunday April got to Sunday school early. She had a frame for Bruce's picture, but Bruce was not there.

"Where can he be?" April thought. "I was sure he'd come early so we could put the picture in the frame before the others arrived. But if Bruce doesn't come soon, everyone'll be here!"

Just then the others started coming in. April hid the frame she had brought under some books.

Everyone was talking when Mr. Thomas came in. April gasped; the teacher was carrying Bruce's painting. "This was outside our classroom door when I got here this morning," he said. "Do any of you know anything about it?"

April started to answer, but Ron beat her. "That's really a neat picture! I wish I could paint like that! Wasn't there a card on it or anything?"

"No, it was just there. I can't imagine where it came from," Mr. Thomas said.

"It's good," Angie said. "I wish I knew an artist like that."

"Maybe he'd look funny," April said. "Then would you like him?"

"Who cares what he looks like if he can paint like that!" Ron said. "I'd just like to meet whoever did it!"

"You already have!" April said. She paused a minute before springing her surprise. "It's Bruce! Bruce

44

Whitman painted that picture for our class! And I've got the frame for it!"

"Bruce?" Ron laughed. "Come on, April, quit kidding! Bruce couldn't do that!"

"Why not?" April demanded. "Because he's poor and doesn't have clothes that are as nice as ours? You don't know what he can do—you never took time to find out! All you saw were his clothes!"

April took the painting, turning it in her hands. "See? Here in the grass at Jesus's feet it says 'Bruce Whitman.' I know Bruce did it—he showed me the sketch last week!"

"Then where is he?" Ron asked. "It's a good picture. I'm sorry I laughed at him. I'd like to know how he did it."

"I don't know where he is," April admitted.

"I do," Mr. Thomas said quietly. "Bruce is in another class. He asked Mr. Aiken if he could change. He's in with younger boys and girls, but he said they might like him better."

"He didn't want to be with us any more," Angie said slowly. "I don't blame him. We didn't treat him very nicely."

"Then let's do something about it!" April said. "Let's do what Jesus would do!"

"Jesus would want us to tell Bruce we're sorry," Ron said.

"And ask him to come back to our class," Angie added.

"We could ask him to paint more pictures," April said. "Maybe some of the church people would buy them. But most of all, we can be Bruce's friends! That's what Jesus would do!"

But if you treat people according to their outward appearance, you are guilty of sin, and the Law condemns you as a law-breaker.

James 2:9

*Lord Jesus, it is so easy to look at people's outward appearance and then look no further. Please forgive me for judging people by the clothes they wear. Help me to look deeper—into their hearts, as you do. Amen.*

# No School

The family was at dinner, each telling what had happened that day at school or work. When it was Vicky's turn, she made a face.

"I wish I didn't have to go to school! Mrs. Harding gets mad sometimes, and the kids are always fooling around! Ben Morris is always teasing me!"

"Are you sure it's that bad?" her father asked with a smile.

"It's worse!" Vicky said. "Now Mrs. Harding is making us write to someone who lives at least a thousand miles away! She had a list of kids we can write to, but I think writing to a stranger is dumb!"

"Write to Lynne Modisher," her older brother, Jim, suggested. "You know her, and now that her family's at that mission station in Alaska, she's more than a thousand miles away. It's still the United States, but Alaska's sure different than here in Ohio!"

Vicky laughed, "Writing to Lynne won't seem like homework! She didn't like having to go to school every day either!"

"You can read Lynne's letters in Sunday school," Vicky's mother said. "That will help people from our church keep in touch with what the Modishers are doing."

When she and Jim had taken care of the dishes, Vicky went to her room. She got out a sheet of her best stationery and a pen. "I'll tell Lynne why I'm writing and tell her she was right about school being a drag! I'll ask about her school at the mission."

An hour later Vicky was surprised to find she had written three pages to Lynne. She got the address from the last church newsletter fastened to the bulletin board in the kitchen and stamped the envelope.

The next day Vicky told Mrs. Harding she had written and mailed her letter. "How long will it take me to get an answer from Alaska?" she asked the teacher.

"I'd think three to four weeks," Mrs. Harding said. "You'll have to be patient."

Vicky tried to be patient, but every day she checked the mailbox as soon as she got home. Then, in just two weeks, an answer came from Lynne.

Vicky waited until the family was at dinner to open it. "Dear Vicky," she read to them, "It was great to get your letter! Your class sounds like fun! I had Mrs. Harding last year, and she's nice. I miss all the kids from my old class. Up here I don't go to school 'cause there isn't any! Mom's teaching some of the real little kids, but there's no one my age. I go to school by correspondence! Really! The state has all these courses that they mail to you. Mom can grade my stuff 'cause she's a teacher, but if she wasn't, I'd have to find someone else, or send them back to the state office to be graded."

"That lucky Lynne!" Vicky said enviously. "She doesn't have to go to school at all!"

"Keep reading," Jim urged. "This is interesting."

"The courses and lessons they send are OK," Vicky read now, "but it's not like a real school, and it's not much fun doing them alone with no one to compare yourself with. I miss having the other kids laughing and talking and joking! There's no one my age to play with, and no school parties or ball games or anything like we used to have!"

Vicky looked up from the letter in surprise. "Why, Lynne really misses school! I think it would be great not to have to go to school and to learn at home instead! When you're done, you can do whatever you want!"

Vicky went back to reading the letter. "The mission work is going well, but slowly. Tell Mrs. Harding I said 'Hi,' and that I miss her. Please write again and tell me all the neat stuff you're doing in school!"

"I can't believe Lynne wrote this!" Vicky said. "She never liked having to go to school! I wish I could change places with her!"

Vicky wrote to Lynne immediately, telling her how lucky she was not to have to go to school. "I bet you learn more too," she ended the letter. "I'd never miss school if I was lucky enough not to have to go."

It was almost Thanksgiving when the first heavy snow came.

"School's canceled!" Vicky's mother told her that morning. "Too much snow for the buses."

"Just like Alaska!" Vicky said. "Lynne said they've had snow for weeks, though. I'm going sledding!"

She got her sled and pulled it to the top of the hill near her home. The police always roped off this area for sledders.

Vicky sped down on her sled. The wind rushed past her ears and over her face. She knew her nose would be red. She rode down the hill all morning, then came back after lunch.

It was on the second ride down after lunch that Vicky heard someone scream her name. She had time only to glance behind her when another sled hit hers. Her sled spun around, out of control, and suddenly Vicky saw a parked car in front of her.

"I can't stop! I'm going to hit it!" Then Vicky felt a hard bump, and everything went black. When she opened her eyes again, she saw a man in orange coveralls bending over her. She still felt as though she were moving. "What . . . where. . . . ?" Her voice sounded hoarse and far away to her.

"You hit a parked car pretty hard," the man said. "You're in an ambulance now. Lie still and we'll soon have you to the hospital where they can check you over. You'll be OK though."

Vicky closed her eyes. Her right leg throbbed, and so did her head.

At the hospital Vicky was wheeled into a brightly lighted room, and two nurses began to take off her clothes. Her mother came in a few minutes later.

"I'm so glad to see you!" Vicky was trying hard not to cry, but she could not help it. Her leg hurt more, and she ached all over.

"We're going to give you a shot, Vicky," one nurse said. "It'll make you sleep."

When Vicky woke the next time she was in a strange bed in a strange room. Her parents were sitting by the bed.

Vicky tried to sit up, but she couldn't. Then she realized her leg was suspended above her. "What's happening?" she asked, puzzled and groggy. "I hit the car, and they took me in an ambulance. . . ."

"You broke your leg," her father said, coming to stand beside her and take her hand. "It's a bad break, so you'll have to be in the hospital a while. But we'll come to see you every day, and so will Jim. Someone will even bring your schoolwork," he added with a teasing grin.

"But I won't have to go to school?" Vicky asked. "I'll be like Lynne, won't I?"

During the next week Jim brought Vicky's schoolwork every day and took back what she had finished the day before.

"You're getting it done in record time," Jim told her. "You've read a lot of library books too."

"It doesn't take long when there's no one else around," Vicky said. "I keep wondering what Ben and the others are thinking about the stuff we're doing. I wish some of the kids could come see me, but they won't let them in because they're not old enough. I miss having them to talk to, and I miss Mrs. Harding explaining things. I won't be there for the Thanksgiving party before vacation either."

"That's rough," Jim agreed. He looked thoughtful but said no more.

The next day Jim was smiling as he came into the room at noon.

"What are you doing here now?" Vicky asked in

surprise. "You're supposed to be in school! How'd you get out?"

"I got special permission. Listen, in a few minutes you're going to get a phone call. It's your whole class! We got a special speaker-phone put in for a half hour so when you talk they can all hear you and they can all talk to you. You'd better think about what you want to ask them!"

"Oh, Jim! That's great!"

When the telephone rang, Vicky was so excited her hand shook as she lifted the receiver.

"Hi, Vicky!" came a shout of many voices. "We miss you!"

The next half hour went faster than any other half hour in Vicky's life as she asked questions about school and the Thanksgiving party and all the people in her class. Then the time was up.

"I've really missed you!" Vicky said. "I can hardly wait to get back!"

She hung up the receiver and lay back on her pillow. "Thanks, Jim," she said. "I'm going to write to Lynne right away and tell her I know now what she's missing. Then, I wonder, could you find out how much it would cost for a telephone talk like this with Alaska? It would be the best Christmas present we could all give Lynne. It would be almost like being back in school for her."

> Some friendships do not last, but some friends are more loyal than brothers.
>
> Proverbs 18:24

*Sometimes I like to be alone, Lord, and sometimes I*

*don't like doing the things I have to do in school and at home. But I need other people—my family and my friends. Help me to understand and appreciate them and to be a friend in return. Amen.*

# Jenny the Shadow

Lisa ran down the steps of the school behind her friend Nanette.

"Oh, that Miss Rager!" Nanette said, laughing. "Did you see her face when we all started up for the pencil sharpener just before the spelling test? She didn't know what to do!"

Lisa laughed. Sometimes, though, she felt a little sorry for Miss Rager. It was the teacher's first year, and she did not look much older than the high school students Lisa saw downtown and in church.

"But it's her own fault!" Lisa told herself now, just as she always did. "Other teachers don't let us get away with things like she does! It's her own fault if we do them! What does she expect?"

"I thought I'd die when she tried to say the first word and Bill made the pencil sharpener go so fast no one could hear her!" Nanette laughed. "What can we do tomorrow?"

Lisa was about to answer when a high-pitched voice called her name. Then a whirlwind in a short skirt hit her.

"Jenny!" Lisa grabbed the small girl who had flung herself onto her. "Where did you come from?"

"Your shadow always finds you," Nanette teased. "She wants to be with you all the time. She wants to do everything just the way you do. She even walks like you!"

"I'm going to walk home with you like I always do," Jenny said. She was only in the first grade. She had lived next door to Lisa since her family had moved to town two months before. Jenny had started tagging after Lisa almost immediately. When she found they would be going to the same school, she had begun walking to and from the building with Lisa.

Nanette called Jenny Lisa's "shadow" and teased Lisa about the smaller girl. But Lisa was secretly flattered that Jenny liked her so much. It gave her a good feeling to know someone thought everything she did was right.

"OK," Lisa said. "What did you do in school today?"

"We're making a farm," Jenny said. "And we played games at recess. What did you do?"

Nanette laughed. "We played 'Skip the Spelling Test.'"

Jenny looked up at Lisa, puzzled. "I never heard of that game. How do you play?"

"It's not a real game," Lisa said.

"It's to see if you can get the teacher not to give

56

you the spelling test," Nanette said. "Know how we did it?"

In a minute she was telling Jenny about having everyone go to the pencil sharpener when Miss Rager began the spelling test.

"The sharpener made so much noise, she couldn't pronounce the words," Nanette said. She began laughing again. "Miss Rager had to say we'd have the test tomorrow."

"But you still have to do it," Jenny said.

"Sure," Nanette agreed, "but this way we have another night to study. Or, if we know all the words, a night without extra homework."

Jenny turned to Lisa. "Did you laugh?"

"Sure," Lisa told her. "When she told some of the boys to sit down, they showed her their pencils. They had just broken the points off! And before everyone could get finished at the sharpener, it was too late to give the test."

"Tomorrow we'll do something else," Nanette said. "After the spelling test. Maybe we'll all drop our books on the floor or start to cough. Then maybe Miss Rager won't have time to give us any homework."

Jenny giggled and looked up at Lisa. "You're smart!"

The next morning Jenny was more quiet than usual as she and Lisa walked to school. They were almost there when she said, "Lisa, tell me about what you did in school yesterday. You know, so your teacher couldn't read the spelling words."

"Oh, Jenny, that's nothing," Lisa said. But as she started to tell the little girl again, she remembered the scene and began to laugh.

During the rest of the day Lisa forgot about Jenny.

She and the others in her class decided to wait until just before lunch and then take turns asking to go to the rest room.

"We can use up at least the half hour before lunch," one boy said, grinning. "OK?"

Lisa hesitated. Miss Rager looked tired this morning, and she had been tense as she started the spelling test. But her classmates were laughing and nodding their heads, so no one noticed that Lisa said nothing.

When the time came, the plan worked well. Lisa raised her hand with the others. She reminded herself it was Miss Rager's own fault if they did things like this.

By the end of the day Miss Rager looked even more tired, and her voice was husky. Lisa was glad when the bell rang and she could leave with Nanette and the others.

"Where's your shadow?" Nanette asked as the girls stood in front of the school. "She's usually here by now." She laughed. "Maybe she's found a new friend to shadow."

Lisa frowned. "She walked with me this morning. I wonder where she is. There are some boys from her room." Lisa hurried to where two small boys were shooting marbles. "Do you know where Jenny is?" she asked.

They looked up at her seriously. "She had to stay after school," one said. "The teacher was really mad at her!"

"At Jenny?" Lisa could not imagine the small child making anyone angry at her. "Why?"

"She made a lot of noise at the pencil sharpener and told us to do it too," the other boy said. "So Mrs. Miller made her stay after school."

"Jenny did that?" Lisa told herself it had nothing to do with what her own class had done the day before, but she was worried.

"Jenny's in trouble," Lisa told Nanette. "It's because of us! I'm going in to talk to her teacher!"

She did not wait for Nanette to reply but ran back into the building and to the first grade room that was Jenny's. She knocked on the door, but there was no answer. Slowly Lisa turned the knob.

When she opened the door, she thought the room was empty. Then she heard someone sobbing. Jenny was sitting in her chair, her head on her arms on the table. The tiny shoulders were shaking.

"Jenny, it's me—Lisa." She hurried to the child and put her arms around her. "What's wrong?"

"Oh, Lisa, it didn't work like you said! I tried to do what you and Nanette said, but it wasn't funny at all! Mrs. Miller got mad at me! She said I had to wait here till she comes from the office. No one laughed at all! It wasn't funny like you said. And now Mrs. Miller's mad at me. And I like her!"

Lisa held Jenny closer. She had liked having Jenny admire and copy her. But she had never thought of Jenny getting into trouble because she tried to be like her! "It's not your fault, Jenny. I'll go tell Mrs. Miller it isn't."

Jenny looked up quickly. She wiped her eyes with the back of her hand. "Would you? Would you tell her I really like her? I don't want her not to like me."

Lisa nodded. "You wait here."

She took several deep breaths as she started down the hall. She was almost to the office when the first grade teacher came out. Lisa swallowed.

"Mrs. Miller, I—can I talk to you? It's about Jenny."

The teacher nodded. "Let's go into this empty room. Now, Lisa, what about Jenny?"

"I—well, what happened today wasn't really Jenny's fault." She did not look at the teacher. "It's—it's my fault. You see, I was telling Jenny about something our class did yesterday, and she—well, she tried it today."

"I thought it was someone else's idea," the teacher said softly, "but I didn't know who."

"The kids—well, they do a lot of things to tease Miss Rager," Lisa said. "Maybe you could—well, help her. Tell her what to do."

"I could," Mrs. Miller said slowly, "but I don't think that will be enough, do you?"

"What do you mean?" Lisa asked. But she had a sick feeling inside; she knew what Mrs. Miller meant. "You think I should tell the kids not to do those things! But they wouldn't listen to me! They all want to do them! I'm the only one who feels sorry for Miss Rager!"

"Are you sure?" Mrs. Miller asked. "Have you asked anyone else? They all think you like doing those things to her too. I think you will find others who feel as you do and who have gone along with the group just as you have—because they think they are the only ones who don't want to."

"I'll try," Lisa said slowly. Tonight she would pray hard that Jesus would be with her, and tomorrow she would tell the whole class that she liked Miss Rager and was not going to upset her any more. Lisa had a good feeling inside now—a feeling she would not be the only one to change tomorrow.

You must be perfect—just as your
Father in heaven is perfect.
Matthew 5:48

*Please, Jesus, help me to be a good example to those who are younger than I am. Help me to remember that you are always with me and will help me to stand up for what I know is right in your eyes. Amen.*

# Helper's Surprise

Alone in her room, Chris brushed her hair and pulled it back carefully. She wanted to look her very best tonight. Tonight Barton Wherling would be speaking at her school, and her class was the host room for the program. All the others in the school had been invited to come and bring their parents to hear Mr. Wherling.

"I can't believe I'm actually going to see Barton Wherling the author!" Chris had told her family at dinner. "I've read every book he's written! And Mrs. Noble says he'll tell all about how he got the ideas for them and how he wrote them and even drew the pictures for them. It's so exciting! I'm going to try to get his autograph!"

Her father laughed. "I don't doubt you will."

"It would be easier if I'd been one of the ones picked to sit on the stage with him," Chris said with a slight frown. "Or even to be an usher. Mrs. Noble put all our names in a sack and picked out the ones to do everything, but she didn't pick my name."

"What will you be doing then?" Chris's mother asked.

"Mrs. Noble said we should just sort of 'mingle.' Afterwards, in the cafeteria, we'll help pass cookies and punch," Chris said. "I'll try to get his autograph then."

"I'm glad the parents were invited," Chris's father said. "And that Grandma could come to stay with Ricky and Charley."

Chris laughed. "I guess when you're only four and two you don't care about hearing Mr. Wherling. But some day when they read his books, I'll tell them I met him in person!"

Now Chris checked herself in the mirror. She whirled around in her excitement and decided she looked just fine—even to meet Barton Wherling.

"I'll see you later," she told her parents as she left to walk to the school. She had to be there early, like the rest of her class, but she would come home with her parents after the program.

At school Chris found everyone as eager as she was to meet the author whose books they had read and liked.

"I can hardly believe my name got picked to sit on the stage with him!" JoAnne said.

"At least I'm an usher," Rick said. "I want to ask Mr. Wherling how he draws those pictures!"

Chris felt a stab of envy. Why couldn't her name have been picked to sit on the stage or usher? But she did not let herself think about it long.

"All right, class," Mrs. Noble said as she took her

place at the front of the room. "We have a bit of a problem. Some of the parents will be bringing smaller children, and, since we have limited room in the auditorium, we will have to put them in a different room. I will be in charge, but I need some help. Do I have any volunteers?"

Chris looked around. No one had raised a hand. No one wanted to be stuck with baby-sitting when Mr. Wherling was talking about his books!

"They should know not to bring little kids!" Chris said. "My parents did! They should get sitters!"

"Some parents can't afford sitters," Mrs. Noble said, "and have no one in the family to do it for them. If they couldn't bring their little ones, they would have to stay home."

"Well, I can't do it," JoAnne said. "I'm sitting on the stage." She looked at Chris. "You're not doing anything special, and you've had lots of experience with your little brothers!"

"But I want to hear Mr. Wherling too!" Chris knew anyone who helped Mrs. Noble with the children would miss the whole program! And she had looked forward to it for so long.

"Never mind," Mrs. Noble said. "I'll see if I can find someone from another class."

Chris gave a sigh of relief. Then she looked again at her teacher. Mrs. Noble looked tired. Chris remembered she had been at school all day and had stayed afterward to get things ready for tonight. Mrs. Noble had looked forward to hearing Mr. Wherling too. Now she had to take care of more children instead.

Chris thought about how little Ricky and Charley needed to be played with and watched when she sat with them. If a lot of children came, Mrs. Noble would be even more tired. And it would be hard to find someone who would give up the chance to hear Mr. Wherling.

"I'll help you," Chris heard herself saying. "Will we use the kindergarten room?"

Mrs. Noble smiled. "Yes, and thanks, Chris. If you want to go down there now, you can get things ready. I'll be there as soon as I can."

In the kindergarten room, Chris turned on the light and began to get out some of the toys. She looked at the clock. It was still a half hour until Mr. Wherling would speak, but parents would be bringing their children in soon. She wondered if Mr. Wherling was here yet.

Chris was looking through the books, trying to choose one to read to the children, when the door opened. A tall man carrying a briefcase smiled at her. Chris did not know him, but he looked strangely familiar.

"Hello," the stranger said. "I'm looking for the auditorium. This is the first room I saw with a light on, so I thought I'd better get directions. I'm—"

Chris gasped. She knew now who he was. "You're Barton Wherling! Oh, you really are, aren't you?"

The author smiled. "I always have been, but how nice of you to recognize me!"

"Oh, I've read all your books!" Chris said. "Most of them have your picture on the back! Everyone's so excited about you coming to our school! We want to hear about how you write your books."

Mr. Wherling smiled. "I'll try to tell you. But how come you're down here and not with the others in the auditorium?"

Chris looked away. "I—I'm going to help Mrs.

Noble baby-sit with the little ones. She—well, no one told the parents not to bring them, so someone has to take care of them."

"And you got stuck," Mr. Wherling said sympathetically.

"Oh, no!" Chris said. "I mean, well, sort of, I guess. I said I'd help because no one else wanted to, and I didn't have any other special assignment, and Mrs. Noble needed help. I didn't want to miss your speech, but. . . ." She did not want Mr. Wherling to think she would rather be here than listening to him!

"But now you will miss it," the author said. Then he smiled. "Not completely though! Look, I always carry a small tape recorder with me—in case I get any ideas for new books—so I'll tape my talk. Then I'll give you the tape!"

"For myself? To keep?" Chris could not believe it. "Oh, that would be great!"

Mr. Wherling smiled. "I like to help someone who is willing to help other people. A lot of people have to help me with my stories and books, and I appreciate it. You're a real helper to Mrs. Noble. I'm sure the little ones will like having you take care of them."

"I guess I never thought of myself as a helper," Chris said slowly. "I just knew Mrs. Noble would like someone else here with so many to take care of."

"You know, you're something like the heroine in my new book," Mr. Wherling said. He opened his briefcase and rummaged in it a minute. Then he pulled out a book. It had a brightly colored picture on the front and the words "The Old Elm Mystery." Below, in smaller letters, it said "by Barton Wherling."

"Is that a new book?" Chris asked. "I never saw it before. They don't have it in the library."

Mr. Wherling smiled. "It's too new. In fact, this is one of my advance copies." He took a pen from his pocket and opened the book. "What's your name?" he asked.

"Chris. But—"

"To Chris," Mr. Wherling said as he wrote. "For being a true helper. With best wishes from Barton Wherling." He blew on the page to dry the ink, then closed the book and handed it to Chris with a smile. "And now I'd better find that auditorium. I'll see you later, Chris, and I'll bring the tape."

"Thank you," Chris managed to say as Mr. Wherling left. "Thank you." She looked at the new book in her hand. "I'm glad I decided to be a helper," she thought. "It's even better than being on stage!"

The door opened and a mother came in with two small children. "Hi," Chris said as she took their hands. "Come on in. We're going to have a lot of fun tonight."

> Help carry one another's burdens, and in this way you will obey the law of Christ.
>
> Galatians 6:2

*I want to be a helper, Jesus, to make life easier for my family, my friends, and for other Christians around the world. Show me how to help them the way you have helped me. Amen.*

# A Job for Teri

Teri's heart was beating fast as she followed Mrs. Johnson through the house. There were plants in every room. When they reached a small greenhouse that had been built onto the house, they stopped. The winter sun came through the glass, making shadows in the room. It smelled like a garden.

"I have numbered each plant," Mrs. Johnson said. "I have a list of when each one should be watered, misted, or fed. If you follow the list exactly, you should have no trouble. Just be sure to come every day, because all the plants aren't on the same schedule. And be sure to check the temperature in the greenhouse each day. If you have any questions, I'm sure your mother will be glad to help you."

"I'll remember everything," Teri said. She did not tell Mrs. Johnson that she had not yet told her parents about getting this job while the Johnsons were in Florida for the next 10 weeks.

Teri was sure she could do the job, and she wanted to buy a nice present for her parents for their anniversary. With the money Mrs. Johnson would pay her, she could do it. But she wanted it to be a surprise.

"Then here's the house key." Mrs. Johnson handed it to her on a small ring. "Don't lose it."

"I'll keep it with me and come in every morning before school," Teri said. She put the ring into her jacket pocket. "I don't usually go to school this way because it's longer, but I'll leave earlier now. I'll follow your list every day."

Mrs. Johnson smiled. "I'll tack the list on the back of the front door. I'll pay you as soon as we get back."

"Thanks, Mrs. Johnson, and don't worry. I can take care of your plants just fine."

The next morning Teri let herself into the Johnson's house. It was almost spooky, walking into a strange house that was empty. It was so quiet Teri could hear a clock ticking.

Teri checked the list on the front door. She felt important as she filled the long spouted watering can and went from room to room. This was her first paying job, except for working for her mother. It made her feel very grown-up as she checked the temperature in the greenhouse.

By the end of the second week Teri was used to the Johnson house and the plants. She did not stand and talk to them like she had the first few days. Now she watered the ones on the list as quickly as she could. She put the house key in her jacket pocket and hurried to school so she would have time to talk to her friends before the bell rang.

70

Thursday morning her best friend, Anne, met her at the school door. "Teri, the greatest thing has happened! Mom and Dad are taking me skiing this weekend, and you're invited too! There's a beginners' slope, and we'll take lessons and everything! Say you'll go—please!"

"Oh, yes! When do we leave?"

"Right after school," Anne said. "We get tomorrow off because of that teachers' meeting, and Dad just found out he can take tomorrow off too! We'll go to church up there Sunday morning and come home Sunday night. Call your mom right now and ask her!"

Teri's mother was surprised but quickly gave her permission. "I'll pack your clothes so you'll be ready as soon as school's out," she promised.

All day Teri dreamed about the skiing weekend. When school was over she hurried to her locker for her jacket. As she put her hand into the pocket, her fingers touched the hard metal that was the Johnson's house key.

"Oh, no!" Teri thought. "Mrs. Johnson's plants! I forgot all about them! I can't water them if I'm away! What'll I do?"

She looked around just as Anne came hurrying down the hall. "Come on!" Anne called.

"I—I can't go." Teri could feel the tears of disappointment coming. She explained quickly about the Johnson's plants.

"Get your Mom to do it for three days," Anne said with a shrug.

"But then they'll know about the surprise! I don't want them to! And I can't give the Johnson's key to anyone else! They wouldn't like that. It could get lost, or—"

"I know!" Anne said suddenly. "Mom has a couple of plants, and when she's going to be gone she just waters them with a lot of water and they take care of themselves!"

"Do you think that would work?" Teri asked doubtfully.

"Sure! Mom wouldn't do it if it didn't work! Come on, I'll go with you, and we can get it done twice as fast and be ready when Dad gets home."

"OK." Teri smiled. "I'm sure glad I don't have to miss going skiing for a few plants!"

In the Johnson house, Teri checked the list. She began watering all the plants that she would have watered Friday, Saturday, or Sunday. When she came to the greenhouse, Anne was coming out.

"I got all the ones in here," Anne said. "Let's go!"

"Right!"

The skiing lessons the next day were fun. By afternoon both Teri and Anne were going down the beginners' slope easily. They skiied all day Saturday too.

When they got up Sunday morning there was a little more snow. They went to church on a big sled pulled by two snowmobiles. It was fun to visit a different church, Teri thought. She was glad, though, that the Bible readings and hymns were familiar. It made her feel at home.

Sunday afternoon they came home. Teri was tired, and she went to bed early. The next morning she went to the Johnson house before school.

She checked the list and began watering the plants. They all looked healthy to her.

"It worked fine," Teri thought. "And I had so much fun skiing. But I won't miss any more days." She even took time to talk to the plants a while.

It was several days later that Teri noticed a brown leaf on one plant in the greenhouse. She told herself it would get green again, but the next day it was worse. The third day it dropped off, and two more were starting to turn brown.

"What'll I do?" Teri thought in alarm. She tried not to think about the plant, but she could not forget it. After school she went straight home.

"Mom, what can you do if a plant gets brown leaves and they start to drop off?"

Her mother frowned. "That depends. Sometimes it's too late to save the plant. What kind is it? And where is it? I didn't know you had any plants."

"I'm not sure what kind it is," Teri admitted. She sighed. "Oh, Mom, it was going to be a wonderful surprise. . . ." She told her mother about the job watering Mrs. Johnson's plants, and how she had watered them ahead when she went skiing. "They looked all right at first, but now one has brown leaves that are falling off!"

"Let's go look at it," her mother said.

Teri let them into the Johnson house. "It's in the greenhouse." She led the way.

Her mother studied the plant and its leaves. "We'll try to save it, but I'm afraid it's dying, Teri. It got too much water. Most plants don't need a lot of water, and you gave this one too much. That's why Mrs. Johnson made that list for each plant."

Suddenly Teri remembered the afternoon she and Anne had watered the plants. "But I didn't do it! Anne did! She didn't look at the list either! She just watered everything in the greenhouse! It's her fault!"

Her mother looked at Teri seriously. "I'm sure you know better than that," she said softly. "Anne might have done the actual watering, but the plants were *your* responsibility."

Teri looked down at the floor. "I know. Oh, Mom, what'll I do?"

"What do you think you should do?" her mother asked.

Teri felt a sick feeling inside. "I'll have to write to Mrs. Johnson tonight and tell her what happened. I'll tell her you're going to help me try to save it. I'll tell her I won't miss a single day from now on. And if the plant dies, I'll buy her a new one from the money she is paying me! Oh, I hope she isn't mad at me! I hope she'll let me keep watering the plants!"

Her mother put her arms around Teri. "I think Mrs. Johnson will be disappointed, but I think she will understand. You have just learned a hard lesson, Teri. When we are responsible for something, we must do what we have promised to do. You forgot that because you had a chance to do something that was more fun."

"And now I won't have enough money for your anniversary present," Teri said.

Her mother smiled and squeezed her hard. "Dad and I will be happy with a card, honey—and knowing our daughter is growing into a responsible worker."

> How happy that servant is if his master finds him doing this when he comes home! Indeed, I tell you, the master will put that servant in charge of all his property.
> Luke 12:43-44

*Thank you, Lord, for all the beautiful things you have*

74

*given us. Thank you, too, for the chance to work to keep these things beautiful. Help me to be a faithful worker in everything I do—for your glory.*

# Fire Drill

Jan burst into the house. "Mom! I made it! I made middle school cheerleader! It was fantastic! I did every routine without a single mistake!"

Her mother hugged her. "I'm glad for you, honey. But you know we'd love you just the same if you didn't make it."

"I know, but I wanted to so much! Everyone in school knows who the cheerleaders are! Even the bigger kids from the high school know! And the little kids from the elementary schools think you're really important!"

"Just remember," her mother said, "a leader has responsibilities too."

"Sure, Mom, I know."

For the next two weeks Jan practiced cheers with the other five girls who had been elected as cheerleaders. Jan liked wearing the uniform to school the day of the first basketball game. She knew the other girls envied her because she was not only a cheerleader but was now captain too.

But just before the second game of the season, Mrs. Hensley called Jan into her office off the gym.

"Have you got some new routines for us to learn?" Jan asked the coach excitedly.

Mrs. Hensley shook her head. "It's something else. I hear you haven't been turning in your homework on time, Jan."

Jan laughed. "It's only been a day late—a couple of times. I just got busy with things—like cheerleading."

Mrs. Hensley did not laugh. "You're a leader, Jan. The others look up to you. They want to be like you. They think what you do is right for them to do too. But being a leader has responsibilities as well as privileges."

Jan stopped smiling. Mrs. Hensley was starting to talk like her mother did!

"You must take your responsibilities as a leader seriously," Mrs. Hensley went on. "One of those is to be as good a student as possible. I don't want you putting off your homework any more."

"All right," Jan said softly. "I'm sorry."

Later Jan complained to her brother, Don, about it. "I didn't know I had to be perfect to be a cheerleader! What's the big deal if I don't get my homework in on time a couple of days? I always do it!"

Don was on the high school football team. "I have the same problem. Coach is always telling us how we should dress and act when we're not in uniform. He says we have to be examples! But I guess he and Mrs. Hensley are right; if the other kids are going

77

to copy us, we have to do the right things. They even notice if we go to church and Sunday school every week."

"I think you're all exaggerating! No one pays any attention to what I do," Jan said.

"Yes, they do," Don said. "The kids in your school would do anything you told them to do."

Jan laughed. "Then I'd better get my homework in on time!"

The middle school basketball season had five games played against other teams from towns near by. Jan loved the away games and visiting new schools. There were never as many of their fans there, of course, but a lot of the parents, teachers, and students followed the team.

The team did well, and by the time the last game came, they were playing for a perfect season. The game was scheduled for evening so all the parents could come.

"It'll be a big crowd for our little gym," Jan told Don. "I wish we could play in the high school. I'd love to cheer there! I want to be a cheerleader when I get to high school. But I guess I'd be even more scared there than I am now. I've never cheered in front of so many people."

Don grinned. "I feel jumpy before a game too, but once you start your first cheer you'll be fine. You do it the same way whether the gym's empty or packed."

Don was right. Once Jan began cheering, the big crowd did not bother her. In fact, it made her feel good. She had never had so many people yelling with her.

The second half had just begun, and Jan and the

other cheerleaders were sitting on their bench, when the girl next to Jan grabbed her arm.

"Look!" Her fingers dug into Jan's skin, making her wince.

Jan looked toward the roof. To her surprise, she saw a wisp of white smoke.

"It's a fire!" the other girl said. The other cheerleaders glanced at them, but the noise of the crowd had drowned out her words.

"Be quiet!" Jan looked for Mrs. Hensley, but the coach had gone for a drink of water. There were no adults near them.

Jan looked at the smoke again. If they did not do something quickly, others would see it too. She had read about how people had trampled each other when they rushed for the doors to escape a fire.

"What'll we do?" The other girl's voice was frightened.

"Fire drill!" The words came out as Jan thought them. "Go ring the fire drill bell! Don't tell anyone except Mrs. Hensley if you see her. But go ring it now!"

The girl hesitated. No one but the principal was supposed to ring that bell. It was connected, too, to the fire station. If they had not received a telephone call that it was only a drill, Jan knew they would come quickly.

"Go on!" Jan shoved her toward the door. "Hurry!"

Jan looked at the smoke again. It was only a little more, and no one had noticed. Everyone was watching the action on the floor. But it could not be missed much longer, Jan knew. There was no time to wait for the fire drill bell. Besides, the parents would not

know what it was or what to do when they heard it. She had to do something right now!

Jan grabbed the megaphone the cheerleaders used and rushed onto the floor. The players stopped in surprise as the referee started toward her, an angry frown on his face. Jan did not wait for him to get to her. "We are going to have a fire drill!" she shouted into the megaphone. "The bell will ring any second, but we can start now! You kids know what to do. Stay with your parents and show them and our visitors how we do it. Start now, top rows of the bleachers first."

"What are you doing?" the referee demanded.

Jan was shaking. "Fire!" she whispered. She shouted again into the megaphone. "Top rows, get moving!"

The students did not hesitate now. They began to do as Jan said. They led their parents and visitors down the steps, and the next rows followed.

When the fire drill bell rang a few seconds later, the spectators were on their way out. Then everyone seemed to see the smoke at the same time.

"Fire!" a voice screamed, and more took it up. "It's a real fire! It's not a drill! Let's get out of here! Let me out of here!"

The referee blew his whistle loudly. In the sudden silence, Jan shouted again. "Keep walking! You kids— don't run! You know how to do a fire drill! Just keep walking, and it'll be all right. Stay with your parents! Walk!"

The two teams and cheerleaders had left when Jan saw the principal pushing toward her through the crowd. "Keep talking, Jan!" she shouted at her. "Keep talking to them!"

Jan started to hand her the megaphone, but she shook her head. "I'll stand here beside you, but they're listening to you. You keep talking!"

Jan did as she was told. "Walk as fast as you can, but stay in line. One row at a time, as soon as the one above you gets past! That's good. Keep walking!"

The smoke was getting thicker now, and Jan heard some people coughing. She did not know what else to say, so she kept repeating her instructions about walking. "Get outside!" she added. "Just like we do in our fire drills!"

Now Jan began to remember the instructions the teachers gave for fire drills, and she repeated them through the megaphone.

"Everyone's on their way out," the principal said. "Let's go too!"

The fire sirens were screaming and two big red trucks were coming into the school yard when Jan and the principal walked out of the gym. In a few minutes the fire chief came out and picked up his bullhorn.

"It's all out, folks! Nothing serious; we'll know exactly what caused it tomorrow. But we got here fast enough to prevent any major damage. Your game will have to be played later, though. You can go home now."

Jan's legs were suddenly weak. She leaned against a parked car.

"You did it, Jan!" The principal put her arm around her. "If the people had panicked, many could have been hurt—or worse. It wouldn't have mattered that the fire wasn't serious if they had begun to push and shove. But when they saw you standing there, telling them what to do, our students did what you told them. They followed your orders and did what they'd learned in fire drills. You're going to be a real heroine! I'm proud to say you're one of our school's leaders."

Jan gave her a tired smile. She was not sure about being a heroine, but she understood now what being a leader meant.

> Whoever wants to serve me must follow me, so that my servant will be with me where I am. And my Father will honor anyone who serves me.
>
> John 12:26

*Sometimes I am the one people follow, Lord. When I am the leader, help me to lead in the right way and for the right goals. Help me to lead others to you and your Word. Amen.*

# Which Way's the Trail?

Lori put the last T-shirt into her duffel bag and zipped it.

"You'll have fun at the nature and outdoor camp," her older sister, Carol, said. "We went there when I was in your grade, and it was great! You learn a lot about nature and stuff, but you have fun too."

"I hope I will," Lori said uncertainly. "I have to be in the same cabin as Sara Snapping Turtle."

"The Indian girl?" Carol asked.

Lori nodded. Sara was a full-blooded Indian from the West. Her parents had died a few weeks ago in an accident, and a family from town who had been sending them money for Sara's school had asked Sara to come live with them.

"She acts like she hates us and everything here!" Lori said. "She doesn't want to be friends with anyone!"

"Have you tried being friends with her?" Carol asked softly. "She misses her parents, and she's in a strange town, far away from people she knows. She's probably not very happy right now."

"You can't be friends with her! She acts terrible! But Kathy Miller's in my cabin too, so we'll have fun."

"Kathy's a leader," Carol said. "Everyone does what she does. If she'd be nice to Sara, the others would be too."

"She doesn't like Sara either," Lori said. She looked at her watch. "I've got to go! Can't be late today!"

At the school, Lori joined the girls around Kathy. All of her cabinmates were together except Sara, who sat off to one side, alone.

"Remember, class," Mr. Knowles was saying, "this is not a vacation! We're getting the chance to spend a week at this special camp to learn about nature firsthand. You'll have fun, of course, but you will all be expected to do your schoolwork too."

"I can hardly wait," Lori said. "My family's camped a lot, but never at this park."

"You call living in a cabin camping?" came a sarcastic voice. "It probably has running water and electricity and maybe even a phone!"

Everyone recognized Sara's voice.

"We're sure it isn't camping to you," came Kathy's smooth reply, and Lori joined in the laughter.

"No, it isn't!" Sara had come over to them now, her dark eyes flashing. "I know how to really live outdoors! I can live without things you have to have—like running water and electricity!" Sara gave them all one last glare, then pushed her way back to where she had been sitting alone.

Lori suddenly remembered what Carol had said

about being friends with Sara. "She misses her parents and her home," she said.

"Home?" Kathy sneered. "A shack with a dirt floor is what she lived in! I think that's gross! And she's always acting like it was better than what we have! What are you taking her side for?"

"She didn't have any choice," Lori started to say, but no one was listening. Their bus was pulling in.

Lori was relieved to get aboard. There would be talking and singing and laughing on the way to the state park, 100 miles north.

At the camp, Lori followed Kathy and the others to Cabin 6. She put her worn sleeping bag on the bunk with her name. Sara had a bedroll of blankets, and Kathy had a new, brightly colored bag. Everything Kathy had brought looked new.

"We'll meet in the dining hall for a preview of what we'll be doing all week," said the young woman who was the counselor in charge of their cabin. "You'll meet all the staff, and then we'll take a short hike around the camp before lunch."

"What's for lunch?" Kathy asked.

The counselor smiled. "Macaroni and cheese, home-made bread, tossed salad, and cookies and fruit for dessert. Dinner's fried chicken."

"You call that camping?" Sara sneered.

Lori sighed. She wished Sara would try harder to get along with the others. It would be a long week this way.

Lori was right. By the third day no one in the cabin was speaking much to Sara, and the Indian girl did not seem to care. Even the counselor looked worn out.

"Let's get the cook to make us box lunches and hike to the top of the mountain to eat them," the counselor said that afternoon. "We'll be back before dark and the campfire."

Everyone looked at Kathy who said, "Great idea!" Everyone agreed, except Sara, Lori noticed.

The counselor noticed too. "Doesn't that sound good to you, Sara?"

The Indian girl shrugged. "I have to go, don't I? So let's get started."

Each girl put the things she needed into a backpack or small bag. Those with canteens filled them with water.

They walked single file along a trail that led through a meadow, along a stream, and then began to climb slowly up the mountain. Kathy was in the lead; Sara at the end. Lori was near the middle, beside the counselor.

They were about a half mile from the camp when the counselor stopped. "I forgot my First Aid kit! I'm not allowed to take you anywhere without it. You all take a rest for a few minutes, and then walk slowly. I'll go back for it and catch up with you. Just stay on the trail."

The girls sat on the ground as the counselor jogged back toward camp. When she was out of sight, Kathy jumped up. "Come on, it'll be more fun by ourselves!"

The trail began to climb more steeply, and Lori started to puff. Kathy and the others were slowing down too. Only Sara was still walking as though they were on level ground. She moved ahead of them.

"Sara, wait for us!" Kathy called.

Sara turned and grinned. "If you can't keep up, it's not my fault! I'll see you at the top!" In a flash she had disappeared around a bend in the trail.

"Smarty!" Kathy shouted. She looked at the others. "Let's catch her!"

"We can't!" Lori said. "She's too far ahead now, and she can go faster! She'll be there long before we are—unless there's a short cut we don't know about!"

Kathy grinned. "A short cut! Sure! Lori's got the idea! If we go over that way, then cut back, we can beat Sara and show her we're as smart as she is!"

"But the counselor said not to leave the trail," Lori protested.

"We'll be back on it before she ever knows! And we'll beat Sara! Come on!" Kathy led the way off the path and into the woods.

Lori hesitated, then as the others began to laugh and follow Kathy, she left the trail too.

They were soon out of sight of the trail, deep among trees and underbrush. Lori was surprised at how much darker it was here, shaded by so many leaves.

"Let's go that way," Kathy said, and led the way. The others straggled slowly behind.

They had gone only a little further when there was a shout from behind them. Sara was coming from the direction of the trail.

"What are you doing here?" Sara demanded. "You were supposed to stay on the trail! When I didn't hear you coming behind me, I came back to see what happened. You're lucky I did! You're just getting lost this way! I know how to read a track in the woods, so I could come right to you, but not everyone could!"

"This is a short cut!" Kathy said. "You don't have to come if you're afraid!"

Sara seemed to freeze. "I'm not afraid of anything

in the woods, but I have sense enough—and respect enough for the woods—not to do stupid things! I'm going back to the trail! If you want to go on and get lost, that's your business! I won't be coming after you this time, so if you're smart you'll come now!"

"Go on!" Kathy said angrily. "We don't need you! Come on, gang, let's go! She's just jealous because we're as good in the woods as she is!"

The others hesitated, and Lori most of all. Sara was right, she thought, they were going to get lost if they followed Kathy. Leaving the trail had been stupid—and going against orders was stupid too.

"Well?" Kathy snapped at them. "Are you following me or that Indian?"

Lori made her choice. "I'm going with Sara." She started after the new girl.

"Me too," said another voice, and then another and another.

"She's scared you all!" Kathy shouted. But as they all started after Lori, she shrugged. "All right, we should stay together!" She stamped after them, scowling.

Lori was the first to catch up with Sara. "We're coming with you."

Sara looked surprised, then smiled slowly. "I didn't think anyone would follow me instead of Kathy. I was worried. You might have had a bad time in the woods; it's easy to get lost there. But I didn't know how to get anyone to follow me. I always say and do the wrong things here. Thanks for coming, Lori."

"That's OK," Lori said. "You're a leader, Sara—just like Kathy is. And most of us are followers. I think you'll have plenty of followers now too. But maybe next time you and Kathy will want to lead us in the same direction."

> And who is he that will harm you, if ye be followers of that which is good?
>
> 1 Peter 3:13 KJV

*We can't all be leaders, Lord. Make me a good follower, one who knows who is leading her and the direction she is going. Make me a follower who can help the leader and the others who follow. Make me most of all a steady follower of you, so that others will see you in my actions. Amen.*

# Gini's Entry

Gini sat very still as Mr. Warner explained about the All-City Sixth Grade Art Contest.

"Last year the winner came from our school," the teacher concluded, looking at Gini with a smile.

Gini wished she could push a button and disappear. The winner last year had been her sister, Brenda.

"And next year the winner will probably be Bobby!" Gini thought unhappily. "How did I get born in between two such good artists? I can't draw at all! I'll embarrass the whole family if I enter that contest! But Mr. Warner says everyone has to have an entry!"

By the time she unlocked the front door that night, Gini was more discouraged than she could remember ever being. "If only Brenda hadn't won first prize last year . . . ," she thought. She felt guilty that she was not happy for her sister, but having a first prize winner ahead of her made it harder.

Gini went into the empty house and wandered to the kitchen. Brenda now went to the junior high school on the other side of town, and their mother usually picked her up on the way home from work later. Her brother was at a friend's house playing.

A note was stuck on the refrigerator door with a banana-shaped magnet. "Gini, please take the apple pie in the freezer to Mrs. Hammond. Her father is coming to live with them, and she can use it for dinner. Love, Mom."

Gini sighed. "At least I'm good for running errands, even if I can't draw or paint like Brenda and Bobby." She put the pie into a box and walked the two blocks to Mrs. Hammond's house.

"Gini! How nice!" Mrs. Hammond looked tired. "Come in and meet my father."

The old man was sitting in a big chair in a little bedroom. A TV set was on, but Gini saw he was only staring at it, not really watching.

"This is Gini Krummel, Dad," Mrs. Hammond said. "This is my father, Mr. Morgan, Gini."

The old man looked at her coolly, and Gini hesitated. Then she held out her hand. "Hello, Mr. Morgan. How are you?"

The old man held her hand only for a second. "How can an old man be?" he snapped.

Gini did not know what to say, so she looked away. Several pictures in frames hung on the wall. She went over to study them. They were not like any drawings or paintings she had ever seen. "Did you do these, Mr. Morgan?"

The old man nodded. "Don't know what they are, do you?"

Gini bent closer. "Why, it looks like you used—"

"A typewriter! That's what I did—I 'painted' them on my typewriter!"

"But how—I mean, they look like—"

"Like real art!" Mr. Morgan finished. "They are! And I don't have an artistic bone in my body!"

Suddenly Gini remembered the art contest. Nothing in the rules said things had to be painted or drawn. Surely she could use a typewriter!

"Mr. Morgan," Gini said eagerly, "could I learn to do this?"

The old man shrugged. "You have fingers, haven't you?"

"I mean, would you teach me? Right away?"

"Hold on now, I'm no teacher. I don't—"

"Please!" Gini explained quickly about the art contest and how Brenda had won the year before. "I can't draw at all! And she and Bobby are both so good. . . ."

The old man looked thoughtful. "So you feel pretty useless." He sighed. "I know how that feels! All right, we'll start right now."

Mr. Morgan's typewriter was on a table against the wall. "Here's paper," he said. "Put it in and set it for 27 spaces to a line. Then go in 4 spaces and make 19 little o's."

Gini did what he said. It looked like a short line of o's to her, not like the start of a picture at all.

"Now on the next line go in 3 spaces and make 21 o's," Mr. Morgan said. When Gini had done it, he went on. "The next line you indent 2 spaces and

make 23 *o*'s. Then go in 1 space and make 25 *o*'s on the next line. Your last line will be 27 *o*'s."

Gini studied the five lines, each one a little longer than the last. It still did not look like anything to her.

"Indent 1 space," Mr. Morgan said, "and make an *o*. Now, skip 23 spaces and make another *o*. Do that on 6 more lines. Then indent 1 space and make 25 *o*'s. Now what do you have?"

Gini followed the instructions, then laughed. "A house!"

Mr. Morgan smiled at her for the first time. "Right. 'Course, a house is easy, but you can do a lot of other things too. Some people even make pictures of people and famous buildings. I have a book. . . ." He opened a drawer and handed her a book. "You want to try some of these? I use different colored ribbons to make the colors right—red, green, blue, purple, brown, and black."

"Oh, Mr. Morgan, do you think I could do it? It wouldn't be like anyone else's entry!"

"Go to it, young lady."

Gini hesitated. "Could I—well, I'd sort of like it to be a surprise. Could I come over tomorrow after school and do some? If you'd help me, I'd learn a lot faster than if I just read the book."

"Well, now, I don't—well, why not? It'll be something different for me to do."

For a week Gini went every afternoon to Mrs. Hammond's house and worked on her "painting" on Mr. Morgan's typewriter. They had decided on a scene with two houses, one red and one blue, a green lawn, and a few trees with green leaves and brown trunks.

Gini had to start over several times, but Mr. Morgan helped her plan the picture in sections, and she soon learned to know where a letter would hit the paper.

At the end of the week, Gini had the picture finished. Unless she looked carefully, she could no longer see the individual letters she had used—they all blended into the whole picture. She pasted the picture onto a piece of colored paper, wrote her name and school on the back, and took it to class the next day. Her hands were shaking as she handed it to Mr. Warner.

The teacher looked at it, frowning. "Gini, what is this?" Then he stopped. "Why, you did it on a typewriter! Gini, I don't know—the rules. . . ."

Gini hoped her voice would not tremble. "There's nothing in the rules that says how the art has to be done. Just 'an original work of art.'"

The teacher smiled. "All right, we'll submit it with the others. Where did you get this idea, Gini?"

Gini told him about Mr. Morgan. "He's done some that are really beautiful. It took him weeks to do them."

"He sounds like someone who should talk to the senior citizens group," Mr. Warner said. "And enter their arts and crafts show."

When all the contest entries were shown to the class, Gini's got the most attention.

"How did you do it?" everyone asked.

"It's easy, once you get started," Gini said. Later, after school, she talked to Mr. Warner, and when she went to see Mr. Morgan that afternoon, she was excited.

"Everyone liked my picture, Mr. Morgan. They all wanted to know how to do it too. Mr. Warner wants you to come to school some day and show our class how to draw on the typewriter. You can bring your pictures too."

"Well, now, I don't know. It's been a long time since I was in school."

But Gini knew the old man was pleased.

"Will you come to the art show with my folks and me Saturday morning?" she asked.

"All right. I'd like to see it."

Saturday morning Gini was up early. She knew she would not win any prizes with her picture, but she wanted Mr. Morgan to see it displayed with the others.

At the big city auditorium, Gini, Mr. Morgan, and her parents walked down the aisles looking for her entry.

"Here it is!" her mother called. Gini hurried over, then stopped. A white ribbon hung on the picture.

"Mom! A ribbon! They said there might be special ribbons—white ones!" Gini bent to read the words on the ribbon. " 'Most Original Medium.' Mom, I got a ribbon! Mr. Morgan, come quick! I got a ribbon!" Gini hugged the old man. "It's all because of you! Oh, thank you! Thank you!"

To Gini's surprise, Mr. Morgan had tears in his eyes as he took her hand. "No, young lady, I should thank you. I thought my days of being useful to anyone were over, but you showed me they're never over if you don't let them be! I'll talk to your class at school, and to the senior citizens, and give talks to other groups. . . ." He smiled at her. "I'm going to be a very busy man, thanks to you."

Gini smiled back. She and Mr. Morgan had both won something with her entry.

Do not reject me now that I am old; do not abandon me now that I am feeble.

Psalm 71:9

*Help me, Lord, to learn from those who are old. They have a lot to teach me. Help me not to envy other people and what they can do, but to find what you want me to do. Amen.*

# Winner's Cup

Kim laid her tennis racket on the ground, then flopped down beside it.

"Kim, you're fantastic!" Her friend Amy stretched out beside Kim. "You beat me every set! I'm still puffing!"

Kim laughed. "I love playing tennis! I'm going to sign up for the tournament at the main playground. I've been practicing for it."

"I bet you'll win!" Amy said. "You're the best player at this playground!"

"But I've never seen anyone from the other playgrounds play," Kim said. "I don't know how good they are. I have to be in the 12-to-14-year-old bracket, and I'm only 12. I'll have to play against older girls. They'll be bigger too."

"But they'll all be beginners," Amy reminded her. "They won't have played any longer than you have."

"That's right." Kim looked dreamily up at the clouds. "I might even win the cup! Wouldn't it be great to have a cup like that to put in your room? Everyone would know you were the very best at something!"

"You'd have your picture in the paper too!" Amy said. "Oh, Kim, it would be fantastic if you got a winner's cup!"

During the next week Kim played tennis every day. She practiced her serving when she was alone, and played anyone who would play her. She also hit balls against the practice wall for hours.

The day of the tournament finally came. Kim and Amy rode their bicycles to the main park and playground across town. There were enough tennis courts there to have a lot of matches going at once.

"There's Mr. Wilson," Kim said, pointing to a tall young man wearing white tennis shorts and a knit shirt. "He's in charge. He signed me up for the 12-to-14 beginners' division. Hi, Mr. Wilson!"

Mr. Wilson saw them and motioned for Kim to wait. He came over carrying a clipboard, with a pencil stuck behind his ear. "Hi, Kim. Look, I have a problem. We only had eight girls sign up in your division, and that's not enough to give a winner's cup."

"You mean I can't play for a cup?" Kim felt tears starting to form. "But I want to play, Mr. Wilson. I've practiced so hard. . . ."

"I know, Kim. But the rules say there must be at least 12 signed up for a division in order to have it included in the tournament. You can still play if you want to though."

"Oh, I do! But how can I if there's no beginner's division for my age?"

"You'll have to go into another division," Mr. Wilson explained. "You can go into the 12-to-14 advanced division, or into the 15-to-18-year-old beginners. There are several 18-year-olds in that one, though. It's up to you, but most of the other girls who signed up for your beginners' bracket either did not sign up or chose to go into the advanced division for your age."

Kim was thinking hard. If she went into the advanced group, they would all have more experience than she did, but that did not mean they were automatically better than she was. But the beginning group would be so much older than she was, they would all be bigger and stronger.

"What are you going to do?" Amy asked.

Kim swallowed. "Go into the advanced division. I want to be in the tournament!"

Mr. Wilson smiled. "Good! I'll put you down. I'll let you beginners play each other to start. Your first match will be in a half hour."

As Mr. Wilson walked away, Amy said, "Oh, Kim, I'm so sorry! You wanted to win a cup so much!" She brightened suddenly. "Maybe you still will! You're good!"

"I'm going to try!" Kim tried not to look at the table where the big winners' cups were sitting. She had never won anything like that, and she wanted to so badly.

Kim's first match was against another beginner who couldn't seem to do anything right. Kim won easily. She also won her second match that afternoon.

"See?" Amy said enthusiastically. "You can still win a cup! There are only eight of you left now!"

Kim was excited too, but she tried not to show it. "It's still a long way to a winner's cup, and I have to play the best players from now on."

Mr. Wilson came over, frowning as he checked his clipboard. "You'll play the first match in the morning, Kim. Against Karen Dominick. Be here at 8:30."

"I will!" Kim said.

"Let's get something to eat at the Snack Shack," Amy said as Mr. Wilson hurried off. "I'm starved!"

"I'd like some lemonade," Kim said. "It's hot out there!"

As they walked toward the refreshment stand, a young man and a young woman, both wearing judges' arm bands, walked in front of them.

"That Dominick girl is something else!" the woman said. "She should take her division easily! I never saw anyone take so naturally to tennis. I want to get her in some real matches next year."

"You really think she could be a pro?" the man asked.

"If she has the right coaching," the woman answered. "It would take some real training, but she's for sure the best in this town. I wanted her to go into the older bracket, but she said it was her last year in this division, so she wanted to stay. She won it last year, and she wants to do it again."

"There are so many players in that division this time," the man said.

The first judge shrugged. "Lots of beginners—no trouble there. They're down to one now, but she won't be able to do anything against Karen. None of them will."

Kim could not look at Amy. Her stomach felt like a bouncing tennis ball.

103

At 8:30 the next morning Kim took her place on the court. She had not slept well; big green tennis balls kept chasing her.

Across from her, Karen smiled. Kim nodded and waited for the first serve. It came, hard and fast. Kim got her racket on it, but the ball went into the net. She missed the next serve completely.

Karen won the first game without losing a point. Kim carried the balls back to her baseline, ready to serve. She gave it her best, but Karen was too good. The two volleyed only once before Karen scored.

The set went on. Kim brushed at the sweat on her face. She had to do better. Then Karen hit a short return. Kim rushed to the net, but failed to get to the ball in time.

"Put your arm out as far as you can," Karen murmured as they ended close together at the net. "You're making your legs do what your arms could— and in less time. Especially on your backhand."

Kim frowned, but as she went back to the center of the court, she knew Karen was right. Mr. Wilson had told her that once too, but she had forgotten it.

Karen won the first set 6-0. As the girls walked around to change sides of the net, Karen smiled. "On your serve, throw the ball a little higher and really reach for it. You'll get more speed on it."

Kim looked at her in surprise. "Really? Thanks!"

Kim's serves did go better during the second set. She won two games, and felt a thrill of pride each time. She lost the set 6-2, and the match was Karen's.

As they shook hands, Kim said, "Thanks for the tips. And good luck the rest of the way. I'll be cheering for you."

104

Karen grinned. "You're a pretty good player now, and next year I think you'll take the cup!"

As Kim came off the court, Amy rushed up to put her arms around her. "Oh, Kim, I'm so sorry you lost! You won't get a winner's cup now!"

Kim glanced over at the cups on the table. The sun was glinting off them, and she knew she would have liked one for her room. But she also knew that even though she had lost the winner's cup, she had not lost everything.

"I learned a lot today," she told Amy. "I learned how to play better, and I made a new friend—one who's going to win the cup! Next year will be soon enough for me to get a winner's cup!"

> We know that in all things God works for good with those who love him, those whom he has called according to his purpose.
> Romans 8:28

*Father, I know I can't win all the time. I ask that you will be with me when I lose, and that you will help me to see that even though I lose, I can find something to "work for good" to help me grow and develop into a better person. Amen.*

# A Beve Original

Beve sat on the floor of the family room, bringing her cousin up to date. She and Marcia had always been close, even though Marcia was in high school. They had not seen each other for a year, but Marcia's family had moved back to town now.

"And then Wendy—" Beve went on.

"Wendy?" Marcia frowned. "That's about the 10th time you've mentioned her and what she said and did. Who is this Wendy, anyway?"

"Wendy Louis. She just came this fall. Her dad was an army officer, and she's lived everywhere—Rome, Paris, Tokyo, and even Manila. A lot of places in this country too. She's fantastic! She knows everything!"

"She's the one who decided you should all wear backpacks instead of carrying your books?" Marcia asked.

Beve nodded. "And she's always planning different

things. Like taking water ballet lessons at the Y, and—"

"Water ballet? You?" Marcia giggled. "You hate swimming! You barely passed beginners! You always swallow half the pool!"

"Well, I'm not very good, but the others all like it," Beve said.

"But you don't like it," Marcia said quietly. She quickly changed the subject. "So tell me about your art. Got any new paintings for me to see?"

"A couple," Beve said. "But I've been so busy lately. . . ."

"You've been so busy swimming and doing other things Wendy wants that you haven't had a chance to paint," Marcia said slowly. "But you love painting and you hate swimming!"

"But Wendy says—"

Marcia took a deep breath. "But you're not Wendy! You're Beve! You're you. You aren't a copy of anyone! God made each one of us an original! You've got to be yourself. Oh, it's great to try new things; we should all try a lot of new things because we may find we like some of them a lot. But when you try something and don't like it, but keep doing it because of someone else, that's no good, Beve."

"But the others want to go, and Wendy only asks special girls in the class to be in her group. If I stop going to water ballet, I won't get in on the other things either."

"It's your life," Marcia said. "But you're acting like it was Wendy's life. Think about what you really want to do with your free time."

Beve forgot Marcia's advice until the next day

when Wendy said, "Let's all go out to the stables Saturday morning and ride horses!"

The others agreed enthusiastically. Beve hesitated. She always cleaned her room Saturday morning so she could paint or read in the afternoon.

"But I can clean it later," she told herself. "I don't want to be the only one who doesn't go with Wendy. And I've never ridden a horse, so Marcia can't say I shouldn't go or that I'm just copying Wendy."

"We'll meet here at the school at nine," Wendy was going on. "Our station wagon will be big enough for all of us."

That night Beve told her parents about the Saturday plans.

"Who'll be driving?" her father asked.

"Wendy's mom or dad, I guess. She said we'd use their station wagon."

"That's fine," her father said. "But you know our family rule—no riding in a car without an adult until you're 16. That's still a few years for you," he added with a smile.

"Sure, Dad," Beve said.

Saturday morning was crisp and clear. Beve hurried into her jeans and plaid shirt. She was looking forward to riding a horse for the first time. Her bedroom, she had decided, did not look so bad. She would clean it quickly this afternoon and still have some time to paint or draw. Maybe she would do a picture of the horse she rode this morning.

Everyone was at the school early, and at exactly nine o'clock the Louis station wagon came around the corner. Wendy waved from the front seat.

Beve started for the car with the others. At the door she stopped. The driver was not Mrs. Louis or

Colonel Louis. It was Wendy's brother, Bill, who was 17.

"Come on, Beve!" Wendy called. "We're leaving! Hurry up!"

Beve swallowed. The others were all in, even Gayle, who had been last, but there was no adult. If she went with them it would be against the family rule.

"I—I thought your mother or father would be driving," Beve stammered.

Wendy laughed. "Bill, she doesn't trust your driving! Come on, Wendy, Bill's a good driver! Mom and Dad didn't want to spend all morning around the stables!"

"But I. . . ."

"She's not allowed to ride in a car without a grown-up," one of the girls said.

"Not allowed?" Wendy laughed again. "Oh, Beve, how childish! Your folks must think you're still a baby!" She laughed once more, and the others joined in. Then Wendy stopped laughing. "If you're coming with us, get in. If you're going to be a baby all your life, then you'll just have to miss all our fun!"

Beve wavered. Wendy's message was clear: come now or be out of the group and its fun. But two of the words reminded her of Marcia: *your life*. Marcia had said she was an original and not a copy of Wendy. And her parents trusted her to obey the car-riding rule.

Beve's whole body was trembling as she stepped back. "I'm sorry, but I can't go without an adult along."

There was a second of stunned silence, then, to

Beve's surprise, Gayle spoke up. "I'm not supposed to either. I guess I'll go back with Beve," Gayle said.

"Well, if you two aren't the babies!" Wendy said. "Go on and miss the fun! Come on, Bill, let's go! We certainly don't care if these babies don't come!"

Beve and Gayle watched the station wagon pull out from the curb with a screeching of tires.

"I didn't know anyone else had a rule like mine," Beve said.

"My parents wouldn't really care," Gayle said. "But I'm scared of horses. I didn't want to go, but I was afraid to tell anyone why. This way I can blame it on my folks!" She laughed. "Thanks for getting me off the hook!"

Beve walked home slowly. "I guess I'll clean my room," she told her mother. She had had to explain why she was back so soon.

"I'm proud of you, Beve, for doing what you knew was right even when the others laughed," her mother said.

"Sure, Mom." Beve did not want to talk about it. She went back to her room and began to work. At the bottom of a pile of things in her closet Beve found the book on watercolors that she had bought at a yard sale just after school started. She sat down on the floor and opened it.

"I haven't had time even to read it before," Beve thought, "let alone try out some of the things it tells how to do. Marcia's right; I'd rather be painting than swimming!"

Beve had her room cleaned and was well into the book when her mother called her for lunch. As she went to the kitchen to eat, the telephone rang.

"Beve? This is Gayle. One of the girls just called

me! Wendy's brother was driving too fast on the way home and got picked up for speeding! They all had to give their names to the police! She said they were scared all the time Bill was driving them out to the stables, and then this happened on the way back! They all wish now they hadn't ridden with him! Beve, I'm really glad you had nerve enough to stay home! My folks would have grounded me for sure if I'd been in that car!"

Beve said a quick, silent prayer of thanks. Then she told Gayle, "I'm going to stop the water ballet classes too. I want to spend my time painting. Water ballet's great if that's your thing, but it isn't mine. And from now on, I'm just going to be myself! Being a Beve original will be a lot more fun than being a Wendy copy."

> If the Son sets you free, then you will be really free.
>
> John 8:36

*I'm glad you made me an "original," Lord. Help me to use my gifts and talents to their fullest. Keep me from trying to copy others in order to be included in the "in" group. Let me use my talents for you and your kingdom. Amen.*